Meg Whitelaw's story started in the seventies when she was born into a single-parent family. She was raised in a working class, conservative community at a time when single-parent mothers were socially unacceptable. She keenly felt the hostility of her peers.

When a seemingly charming male entered her life at the age of eleven, she believed that fortune had smiled down on them. Never did she imagine that their saviour was a narcissistic abuser who was to subject them to a long reign of psychological tyranny, which they came to know as cohesive control.

Her story is one of survival despite crushing rejection and the pain of betrayal.

Meg Whitelaw

PERILS OF EDEN

AUSTIN MACAULEY PUBLISHERS™

LONDON • CAMBRIDGE • NEW YORK • SHARJAH

A CIP catalogue record for this title is available from the British Library.

ISBN 9781398401532 (Paperback)
ISBN 9781398401549 (ePub e-book)

www.austinmacauley.com

First Published (2021)
Austin Macauley Publishers Ltd
25 Canada Square
Canary Wharf
London
E14 5LQ

I would like to thank Austin Macauley Publishers for taking a chance on a new author.

Table of Contents

Prologue

Germany on the Rhine school trip was to be a defining week in my young life, though I wasn't to realise it until I looked in the hotel mirror and clocked an outburst of spots on my once perfect complexion. Spots which would last a lifetime and I would come to loathe for all they represented: an uncontrollable, adult body. I had thought my first school trip was bad enough when I nearly got whisked away by the ghost of a nun in my faeces-soiled pants. Then there was another ill-fated holiday to Spain when my mother was in danger of being captured by the white slave trade. I should have learned my lesson then and stayed home.

Whilst standing in front of the gleaming, serpentine stretch of water called the Rhine, I felt no delight at the antiquated cobbled roads of Koblenz, nor the thrill of adventure. My only feeling was one of surging horror rising from my loins to my dry throat.

At fourteen, the blood ran down my legs to indicate my encroaching and very unwanted womanhood. I had always dreaded this awful moment as I got slowly thrust into a body I didn't want, a grown-up body which blossomed in comic contrast to my childlike mind with all its childish terrors.

The pimples suddenly bursting out on my nose was an

omen of the emotional turbulence which lay ahead as I landed into menarche with a violent crash. Menarche ought to be the first sign of potential life, but for me, there was only a recognition of the horrors which puberty was about to thrust me into.

Even as a child, I had known that I didn't want children; I didn't want the responsibility especially if the child turned out like me: unfriendly, sullen and uncommunicative. A child no one wanted and no one understood.

To make matters worse, I was on a school trip in Germany and was sharing a room with my mate and two strange girls. I panicked at the thought of them discovering my bleeding shame. How they would point and laugh at the year outcast oozing blood in front of them. In the autumn, they would return to school and tell everyone about the class idiot unable to keep herself clean.

I desperately stuffed toilet roll into my knickers since I was too ashamed to ask a teacher for sanitary towels and couldn't find a chemist in Koblenz. I regretted my inability to speak German because there must have been some shop selling sanitary products.

In spite of using a quarter of a toilet roll, the blood managed to soak through my pants to both my trousers. Its stains taunted me for the rest of a traumatic week.

Seventies Stinger

The seventies started badly for all my family after the peace and love decade of the swinging sixties gave way to the irresponsibility and family breakdown, which was the legacy of a decade wantonly extolling the dubious virtues of free love.

After my parents' acrimonious divorce, my mother was forced to return home to south Wales to her mother, dad and younger brother, whereas her ex made a new family with his second wife.

This had come as a bad time for my gran, who had just lost her mother, who she had lived with in the same village most of her life. The death of my great-gran brought about a period of such intense grief for Gran that she wore black for a year after the death.

On top of this prolonged mourning period, Gran had to deal with my heartbroken, pregnant mother, who had lost considerable weight throughout the pregnancy because of her knowledge that her husband was cheating on her and planning to leave her before the birth.

As it turned out, he had never loved or nor was he even capable of love. Her illusion of their mutual love had been just that an illusion created by a charming deceiver, who was loathed by his own mother.

As the pink-tinged sixties faded away into the harsh reality of the seventies, love had given way to an all-consuming heartache, which was to cause me a difficult birth at exactly 12.30 am—the witching hour.

My mother's return to the village of her childhood was not without its benefits; it was a close-knit community back then with her granddad living just down the road from her mother in a terraced house.

The terraced row had been built at the turn of the last century. The builders didn't bother walling in the co-joined attics, which made the street a haven for thieves. A thief could simply walk into his neighbour's attic, jump through their trap door and leave the house with stolen goods through a back window.

This criminal activity did not cause discord within the community, in fact, it became a long-standing joke in the village that one's neighbours were in one's house while one was out. Everybody knew everyone because they had been brought up together and even worked together, so there was no place for any lasting resentment.

Mum's uncle, Rhys, had always lived there without any desire to leave the valley. Bachelor Rhys was a miner working in the same mine as his neighbours, who had been born in the house in the twenties and lived there all his life as a singleton. Rhys was a timid man with a small circle of friends and with an emotional immaturity which could have been the result of being the younger brother of two sisters.

Lyn, the middle sister, had long ago left grammar school to work as a manageress of a bar which was close enough for her to return home to her family every weekend. Her bedroom had been unchanged since her childhood as was the rest of the property which looked like an Edwardian time warp, apart from the Welsh dresser.

Carpenter great-grandad had handmade the Welsh dresser, which had a Victorian style which stood out amongst the early twentieth-century furniture including a grandfather clock chiming noisily in a corner above the chatter of a house full of parents, their children and their visiting grandchildren.

The only quiet space in the house was the front room or parlour, which had been a study room for Lyn whilst she had attended grammar school (the only child in the family to receive an education after the 11+ exam).

The parlour, in spite of its loneliness since Lyn left home, was actually the most important room of a property which had been devoid of a bathroom until 1970. It was a sort of showroom for the street outside or rather a display room for the neighbours. It was stylish within a limited budget and included a cabinet covered with opulent looking crystals which were there just to give out a statement to the rest of the street:

'We are humble, yet dignified in an understated manner. We may live in a terraced house, but we still have our pride.' Of course, the living room was a different story with its steel bathtub pitched against a fire-belching out coal dust, and its window facing a wall, which darkened the whole room even on the brightest summery days.

The backroom or kitchen beyond the gloom of the middle room was brighter since it looked out onto an extensive garden, and in Great-Gran's lifetime would have been alive with the smell of fresh-baked bread alongside the less appealing aroma of boiled pig's head freshly removed from the body of the family pig killed by the local butcher.

The pigs had to be kept separately from Rhys's vegetable patch which comprised of peas, lettuces, cabbages and two rows of kidney beans. Rhys had become the family breadwinner upon his Dad's retirement; he even owned a rifle for his weekend pursuit of shooting hares with one of his few mates on one of the many mountains cushioning the deep-set valley.

The garden was even big enough for an outside toilet, which was used in the day before the seventies' indoor bathroom, whilst an upstairs commode relieved any nocturnal bladder gripes.

If you were lucky, you would find toilet paper in the outside toilet at the start of the week. As the week come to a close, and the weekly budget began to run dry, the house matriarch had to improvise with newspaper cut into squares large enough to cleanse the average backside.

Gran's upbringing in poverty made her resourceful, as it had sometimes required sacrifices from Gran, who had been a talented clothes maker but was forced to leave school at thirteen to work as a maid. Gran, even when married into a family of four, kept her self-sacrificing nature and became the villagers' unpaid taxi service as soon as she acquired her first car in the seventies. The car was a mini, which at that time was the cheapest car on the road.

This was quite liberating in a village where no one owned a telephone until the seventies; instead folk relied upon the public telephone, which would ring out until a passer-by answered it and looked for whoever the caller wanted to speak to, who would be a neighbour or family member.

Before the seventies, no one in the village owned a car,

and the village was so isolated that any car coming into the village would have attracted the attention of the entire street. Folk would have been at their front doors eyeing up the stranger with naive curiosity. Pre-seventies, the transport in that area was limited to the Swansea bus and my uncle's motorbike. My mother rode on its backseat, and whilst her brother was driving down a back road, which wound passed the river, he lost control of it. The bike slid down the river's bank and landed on my mother's back leg. My mum's miniskirt-adorned leg was unprotected from the burning brand logo which pinned it down with a merciless zeal, and the burn travelled through flesh to her bone. The student doctors at the local hospital bandaged the wound without cleaning it first and weeks later when Gran inspected the injury, such was her shock that she took my mother straight to a herbalist in the next village, who used tweezers to remove the fresh skin growing over the festering poison beneath it; she did so without pain killers.

Later, the woman informed Gran that another day and she would have refused to treat Mum's injury because she would have lost the leg, and the herbalist would have blamed by the same incompetent doctors.

This event in Mum's life should have provided her with a valuable life lesson regarding the fallibility of authority figures who our family had always treated as their superiors. I guess childhood programming once installed as a child into one's hard drive is difficult to erase, and it would take decades for Mum to finally question any doctor's decision making.

Anyway, back to the seventies, which—for my family at least—lacked the glowing lustre of the glamourous sixties. The early seventies had heralded the first divorce in the family, the death of a benign matriarch, and the mid-seventies saw the death of her husband; all of which left Rhys on his own for the first time in a house which had once contained five. Rhys lost no time in moving out of his back bedroom and into the front bedroom, once occupied by his parents.

Rhys even moved into the bed upon which they had both died and kept all their Edwardian furniture. I never understood why Rhys didn't change the bed, but maybe sleeping on a mattress full of history made him feel close to the memory of his parents.

There was certainly no way he was moving out of the property either because of memories or the familiarity of a place he had been born in; he was like a wallflower, which had taken root in a safe corner of some daunting garden, where it remained unseen and unmolested by the challenges of what lay beyond its restricted patch.

My mother, on the other hand, was forced to leave her parents' home around the same time for a council property in the next village a mile up the road. This property did not become available to her by chance. Rather a council worker visiting Gran's home took pity on her plight and put in a word for her to the council, which meant she was moved up the waiting list.

Another stoke of good fate was that we were moved next door to the daughter of my Gran's neighbour. My Gran's neighbour was the only English person in that village, but Gran and she shared a love of gardening, and Mum got on well with the woman's daughter.

Alas! Mum soon fell out with an elderly neighbour on her other side, who disapproved of a single parent next door. The brewing situation came to a head when Mum had workmen fixing her roof one afternoon.

'What are those men doing there?' neighbour enquired.

'They are fixing my roof.'

'Trollope!' neighbour spat assuming some other reason for their presence.

'You bitch!' Mum retorted indignantly.

My Mother's ire was irked less by the implication of sexual misconduct and the more by the fact that she did not even want another man; she was still grieving for the loss of her first love, who was no such thing except in her imagination.

The reader would be right to believe that my mother had been shockingly naive in her failure to detect all the red flags of an errant husband. Flags which must have been flying at full mast right above her head.

In truth, her naivety was not really her fault considering where she was raised, in a part of the valley which resembled most folks' idea of Eden. If there was a Tree of Knowledge there, it remained unpicked; if there was a snake slithering through the idyllic pastures, it remained unnoticed.

In other words, there was no knowledge of evil in that village at that time; it had been so isolated that folk there were the last people in Britain to get a TV, mast in the late fifties.

My family had even been raised by my foolish great-gran to see everyone has essentially good, which I am convinced was the virtue which first attracted my mother's husband to her. Her innocence is what brought an emotional trickster into her life. Of course, there is a fine line between innocence and foolhardy ignorance.

Even broken innocence did not stop her from mourning for a lost love, or rather the illusion of it for decades to come.

Her new home soon turned into one pervaded by grief, and I became a crying baby, who shrieked all night. I had undoubtedly picked up one, either the misery of my prenatal state or my post-birth circumstances of being raised by a depressed mother.

My mother did seek help for her malady once when she visited a counselling group in the nearby town. Unknown to her, the local gossip frequented the group just to listen in to the clients' various mental health problems. My mother's support network came to an abrupt halt when she found out that her woes were being peddled around town by a spiteful nosy parker.

However, salvation once more returned to her life when Gran moved into the same street as her in the late seventies: Gran was living just a few doors down from her along with her youngest son now in the mid-teens.

Gran's back was facing a sheep's field, and Gran loved feeding the sheep, who soon learned when it was feeding time. The sheep were always punctual for their midday feeds, and Gran treated them more like pets than farm animals.

Gran's move was crucial to Mum's mental health which was being stretched to crisis point by loneliness. My mother once had a wide circle of friends in the close community; all of whom were married, and none of them wanting a divorcee around their husbands. They had all dropped away from her like rats evading a cat, who might pounce and get its claws stuck into their partners.

At this point, I ought to clarify something about the Welsh extended family because while my grandparents, close by, did provide much-needed support to both of us, there was also an element of control. My gran was obsessively clean, and one time even emptied our coal shed of coal so that she could clean out the inside of the coal shed before refilling it with dust strewn coal. My mother never requested any service from Gran (other than babysitting when she eventually got back to work), yet Gran would do unnecessary work even against Mum's will.

Gran would clean out her own coal fire's ashes every evening after my grandfather got back from his mining job, which traditionally in our valley was a man's job. Gran's attitude was that she could do a better job than anyone else, in which case, she didn't need anyone's permission to go ahead and interfere.

The only time Gran stopped for a break was at lunchtime when all the housewives in the street would gather on a wall outside her drive for a daily afternoon gossip. The sight of a wall full of chatting women with their cups of tea every day gave the street a community feel. The neighbours were all friends, and Gran would even pop into the widow of the next-door house every evening for a cuppa. Everybody on the street knew all their neighbours, who were all working-class, white and Welsh.

Gran's arrival coincided with my primary school attendance in an Edwardian school, which had been attended by my mother, grandparents and great-grandmother, and it was around this time that it was becoming obvious that my anxiety issues were not teething problems.

My first day at the school did not bode well, and neither of the two primary teachers could stop me bawling as I entered an unfamiliar environment which I can only describe as threatening.

The field surrounding the school was picturesque with its

corners of evergreen trees. These trees hid a secret batch of magic mushrooms, which older kids would harvest at dusk during the autumn months. They were a strange sight as they ran around in the dusky field claiming to be able to see gnomes dancing about in the grass.

I was fine until I entered the partial darkness of the windowless hall with the sound of kids playing in the distance, noises which were unfamiliar. The unfamiliarity rattled me. Of course, it didn't help that at the entrance of the school we were greeted with a life-size statue of a Welsh dragon, whose gaze flew on everyone entering the front door. Its fierce stare bore into me and unnerved my four-year-old mind.

The dragon (which in the Welsh language is a feminine word just like kitchen and wife) seemed ill at ease in its gloomy captivity. My mind eye imagined it roaming the school field before jumping the field's fence to enter the meadow beyond and beyond the woody meadow towards the boundless freedom of the mysterious mountains where folk sometimes disappeared never to be seen again.

I even remember wearing a blue dress with a red apple tree on its breast, which the nursery teacher climbed with her gnarled fingers as if she thought that was going to comfort me. I could not be consoled as I was dragged out of the comfort zone of my house into a noisy environment which I interpreted wrongly as hostile.

I was never to settle into that nursery, or indeed primary school; I was even allowed to merge into the nursery corner by the nursery staff, neither of whom were qualified, and both of whom owned their careers to their fathers who knew the school's headmaster. Corners became my refuge as they allowed me to watch the kids' games from a safe distance. There were role-playing games which I didn't understand, and then there were the physical games in the playground which I could not participate in because of my clumsiness and my wonky spine. The one time I had attempted a somersault with the aid of another kid, I felt a sharp pain in my upper back which lasted for a few days later. My lack of understanding and inability to play was to be the start of alienation which was to last for the rest of my school career such as it was.

At four, I was already so miserable that I was skipping out at lunchtime and risking crossing busy roads back to our old village, which I still have memories of as a toddler. There must have been a sense then that I did not belong in the school with happily playing kids while I looked on miserably.

My escapes soon stopped after a row from one of the nursery teachers, and once more, I was forced to hang around playground corners like some sort of spectator in life, who was doomed to look on at life's participators, which was for me a situation which I was desperate to escape if not physically then at least mentally.

Luckily, my over-developed imagination came to my rescue, and increasingly, I sunk into its comforting embrace. My imagination was protecting me from reality and, quite possibly, saving my sanity.

I was comforted by my imaginary persona as a gifted dancer, though my mother, who lived to face the school was soon aware that I was the school loner, which was a new worry for her on top of all the others.

By this time, Mum had been forced to seek out part-time employment since her £8 welfare benefits were keeping us in the instant mash and tinned tomatoes and little else.

The only variation in my diet was my gran's roast beef Sunday lunches and her occasional beef stews and Welsh cakes (thankfully, I preferred savoury food to sweets).

I can't complain of malnutrition though, because up to the age of six the school was still providing a free bottle of milk for each child daily. We were the last generation in Britain to enjoy this luxury in an era when the milkman was still providing the valley's milk and skimmed milk was unheard of. Despite receiving full fat daily, there was only one fat child in our class, who was the farmer's daughter.

The benefits of school milk I cannot underestimate as it gave me a lifelong love of all kinds of milk: creamy, skimmed, soy and almond, which can take credit for my filling-free mouth today. Far from causing weight gain, my lifelong love of milk meant I never developed a taste for fizzy drinks, which would have corroded my teeth and made me more susceptible to middle-aged spread.

Even though I loved dairy products, vegetables and fruit, I couldn't abide any mints and would brush my teeth without toothpaste rather than use a minty toothpaste.

You might be thinking I was a fussy eater, but one night after my night lamp's battery leaked over the windowsill of my bedroom, I got out of bed to lick up all the battery acid from the window ledge. The battery's liquid tasted vile but I was compelled to lap up every last acrid drop.

I had no idea at the time what mental dysfunctional forced me to act out such a bizarre whim and only found out just recently that there is a name for the condition which makes certain children eat objects e.g. carpets which are not only inedible but also pose a health hazard. Pike's disease is a little known condition.

My dangerous eating habits were the least of it for my mother, who was so worried about my inability to mix that she confronted the school Head about it. The school Head, a chapel man, quickly blamed her for my social anxiety, which upset my mother so much that she contemplated taking me out of his school and met up with the Headmaster of a school a mile away.

As soon as she left his office that headmaster contacted my Head to let him know what Mum was planning; it was apparent that the two men knew each other well, which meant that my Head would probably inform his friend that my mother was a troublemaker who was causing my problems.

To be fair, to my Head, my issues were social rather than academic: my reading in primary school was above average, and my only academic hurdle was writing certain numbers, which was linked with my eye-to-hand coordination problems when it came to ball playing. Nobody understood anything about coordination at this time in history, and the teachers probably thought I was lazy when it came to writing.

If my teachers were unsupportive, it was because they had been taken on unqualified by an eccentric Head. Our Head was usually eccentric in a fun way such as on St David's day (March 1st). This was the day on which all us girls dressed up in our Welsh costumes, complete with a tall, black hat without the pointy end, and our Welsh dolls, whereas the boys just wore a real or fake leek.

In the morning, the entire school was taken out into the yard for a photo of us outside the school front, and it wasn't until looking back on the collective photo years later that I noticed that there was only one black child in the entire school. The photo represented (in the seventies and early eighties) a village which was 99% white and the only outsiders would have been English, working class. The English would have blended in easily to an area which had been English speaking since my gran's childhood (my gran spoke Welsh at home but was not allowed to speak it in her village school). My gran's generation seldom bothered to pass on Welsh to their kids in the belief that it was a dying language.

The effect of this education policy, which was Victorian in origin, was that she was neither efficient in her mother tongue nor the enforced language. This meant that Gran's English vocabulary was limited to symbolic speech rather than the usage of the proper words. For example, instead of utilising the words, humiliation or belittling, she would come out with: making you look small.

Maybe, this was a result of a right-side dominated mind, which was more visual in operation than rational, since Gran's outlook on life was always idealistic to the point of being unrealistically romantic regarding the true nature of this world. It might be slightly unfair to blame a school system for her diminished capacity in both languages.

Despite Welsh being a minority language, we all felt Welsh on St David's Day, especially in the afternoon when our Head held the leek eating competition in our school assembly. This involved volunteer lads clambering onto the stage in front of a table loaded with leeks (the significance of the leek being its connection to the saint, who grew them in his monastery garden). The boy who consumed the most leeks won a bar of chocolate. I don't remember how many leeks he munched, but I recalled the Head's harpist daughter playing the harp as he did so, possibly to drown out the gasps of boys whose throats must have been on fire. The harp, as far as I know, has no relevance to the saint and is a Celtic instrument, which Wales has no real claim to. Nevertheless, I lapped all the appropriated culture heaped onto us by our eccentric Head.

The Head's tales were peculiar, too, and sometimes revealed his warped views on women, such as the women he had known in his youth. This woman was apparently a lunatic because she was under the influence of the lunar cycles. In other words, a full moon affected her behaviour in a dramatic way.

As an adult, I can confirm that I become slightly more agitated during a full moon, but as a child, my feverish imagination conjured up visions of a crazed woman tearing off her clothes and running around the countryside nude under the malignant beam of a ripe moon, followed closely by a wondering werewolf like the ones in the horror films. I certainly didn't link his sexism to his dismissive attitude towards my mother.

To be fair, to our Head, he never caned any naughty girl for any misdeed no matter how serious. Maybe, this was due to misguided chivalry on his part, but in morning assembly, it was only the boys who got disciplined. The punishment of his strikes was light and painless; I guess the intention of the public spectacle was more about making a statement to the rest of the school. If the rogue lads found it embarrassing I don't know, but it was certainly entertaining to watch.

Most of the time, I was capable of amusing myself by immersing myself in my own fantasy realm, and by the age of seven, I was writing short stories in the classroom. At that age, I was wearing a high-collared Oriental style nightdress, which inspired me to write a story about a Chinese girl. The teacher liked my story, yet that was the only time I received praise from her. In her annual school report, she gave a C in geography despite my 90 scores (I was top of the class) and complained to my mother about my unfriendly manner in the classroom. The labels of unfriendly, aloof and arrogant were going to follow me from school onwards. Yes, I agree I was friendless up to seven, but this was about to change at least for a short period in my detached life.

I ought to point out that up until I got friendly with my neighbour's kids I was not a lonely child. This might seem like a surprising statement to make coming from an only child who could not engage with her peers. However, God had blessed me with a family a minute walk away from my door, also my mother was taking me to a Sunday school at the local chapel.

The Sunday school idea was for her to meet up with an old school mate whose daughter also attended. I don't remember speaking much to her daughter, who was in my school class since her middle-class background had instilled into her a confidence which I couldn't even contemplate projecting. My only adult examples were women humbled by their impoverished upbringings, which had prepared them for a life of servitude. Not that it mattered to me since I was comforted by an over-heated imagination which provided me with a company of sorts. My companions would never deride me in spite of my eccentricities.

My ability to read at six meant that I could furnish my fantasy life with characters other than my own central character in my own self-created narrative, although none of these characters was other kids. My characters were friendly bears, dogs and living dolls. This makes perfect sense when one considers that I was not relating to children in any way, which from primary school onwards were becoming increasingly hostile towards me, both verbally and physically.

My books, from a local library, frequented weekly by my mum and me, drove me further into my introverted world in two respects: they boasted my over-indulgence in fantasy, and I came to long for the privacy of the children's corner of the library, which was always empty in the evening. After schooldays, stuck in with noisy brats, I appreciated the enforced silence of the library. I was in the one environment where I was actually allowed to be silent. Even at that age, I was showing the tendencies of a recluse as I looked for shelter away from a world which I didn't understand and, at times, was terrifying to my overloaded nasal and auditory senses.

The only sense I enjoyed was my sight as I tended to get fixed on certain objects. These were usually shiny objects such as runner beans, which were small enough to hide in my nappies as a thieving toddler. My theft was quickly discovered when my bulging nappy started to weigh me down.

A few years later, my object fascination graduated to clear crystals which reflected the spectrum of rainbow colours. My object fixation was sometimes strange pictures, such as my gran's desert painting, which hung by her front door. There were paintings all over Gran and Mum's home, yet bizarrely I got fixated on this painting of a barren desert devoid of all signs of life. Its only remarkable feature was its central sandhill casting a monstrous shadow over the sand plains.

Then it struck me, I liked its desolation, its stillness, its lifelessness even its nothingness. An emptiness, which would have repelled others actually attracted me.

I never really got fixated to any of my toys apart from my dolls house, which resembled my desert in its empty privacy. I imagined myself shrinking to fit into its rooms where I could escape from the world outside its plastic walls. My desert and my dolls house—like my books—provided me with an escape not so much into a brighter arena but a hidden dimension where no bullies could reach me. Away from their judgemental gaze, I could be myself. The gaze of derision got to me as much as the taunts: 'You are a freak in our eyes.' The gaze told me.

Considering all this, it is a wonder I managed to befriend two younger kids on my street, but they somehow accepted me for what I was possibly, because they, too, strangely lacked friends. I say strangely because Garth and Cerys were nothing like me.

Luckily, they liked games which I didn't find challenging such as hide and seek and what's the time Mr Wolf. We were a rowdy trio, and never once did I feel ill at ease with them.

I have Garth and Cerys to thank for my love of nature because it was them who got me briefly out of books and into, first, the school field, then a meadow where we picked bluebells, one fine spring afternoon.

My fondest memory of them was one Saturday when Mum decided to take the three of us to a secret beach, which was hidden away behind a forest twenty miles from our home.

My mum was working evenings in a local club, where women were not allowed to play bingo and would remain downstairs whilst the men played upstairs. This gender segregation was the rule (at that time) in all-male committee-run clubs in that area. The women never complained about it, and the word sexism was never uttered.

My mother ignored all the come-ons from the married drinkers because it provided her with a second-hand car and gave Garth, Cerys and me a memorable day out at a magical beach.

The beach was like no other I have been to since; we had to walk half a mile on a sand-strewn path consisting of attached logs until we reached six-foot sand dunes. The excitement overwhelmed me; it was a miniature version of my desert. The beach was even empty apart from us. I found out later that it was the locals' best-kept secret, and rightly so. For the whole day, we had the whole beach to ourselves.

We explored every luminous cranny for washed-up starfish and dried up crabs. Even though it was my shimmering desert, I didn't mind sharing it with Garth and Cerys; I was finally out of my self-contained world which I had once guarded so jealously.

A year later, disaster struck causing my invitation into normality to be snatched away by a misguided decision of Garth and Cerys's mother. Their mother had decided that Cerys was getting too close to me emotionally. Yes, it was true that Cerys had no mates apart from me because, like me, she was so passive that she was unable to defend herself against bullies.

Maybe, her mother was right to be concerned about our bonding at the exclusion of her own peer group, although the decision she made was to backfire on her daughter. The woman banned Garth and Cerys from seeing me again in the belief that they would seek out a wider circle of friends.

Her plan worked for Garth who did find a group of mates, but Cerys just ended up tagging along with classmates she couldn't fit in with. As for me, I had no intention of trailing behind girls who had made it clear that they loathed me, and I couldn't even play their games anyway.

However, this act of unintended cruelty did teach me one thing about myself: like my mother, I bore grudges for any perceived slight. It was our only shared, trait as my mother was as feisty as I was docile. I never raised my voice like she did, and most of my anger, back then, was so suppressed that it would take an incident of physical force to release it.

Most of the time, though, my buried anger was vented in my fantasy life in which I was able to take my revenge against Cerys for robbing me of a promising friendship, which had forced me temporarily out of the fog which was my introversion.

Although I was already a committed introvert by the age of seven, I had still made progress in the real world, which meant that the prospect of crawling back into my lonesome, fragile husk was to be painful. I was like a hermit crab, who had gently stroked its pinchers onto the warmth of the seaside before some thoughtless hand slapped them back into their shell. I crawled back into my inner realm with a resentment stoked in me by the injustice of losing what had been promised to me but had never really belonged to me, a normal childhood. From then on, it was to be just me and my books which were stacked neatly on my immaculate shelves because I was an orderly child, who so detested disorder that I would avoid walking on pavement cracks. I just knew that they shouldn't be there and were an affront to order in my uncluttered domain.

My books were always in their rightful place as were all my toys and my disco music cassettes. It was the seventies, after all, and the film, Saturday Night Fever, had given me a new interest besides books. When Mum bought me cassettes and a Walkman (remember those), I played them every night in bed to ease my nightly insomnia. My insomnia was to become a permanent problem with only books and music as a respite from its torturous grip on my night hours.

My books take the credit for more than just filling up lonely nights because my proficiency in reading may possibly have saved me from entering the remedial class at seven, despite my struggles with multiplication and division.

The remedial class was actually a portable cabin hitched up on stilts outside of the main building; it was the sole cabin on the school site which made its presence on the playground out of place, especially as its starkly grey walls were pitched next to grainy, Edwardian stone.

The cabin, looking back, gave out an unintentional, but a symbolic message to the rest of the school regarding the kids in the cabin. These kids were not labelled 'special needs' in the seventies; they were remedial kids at best and spastics at worse. Either way, their difference was a negative one, which was symbolically highlighted by the presence of a cabin positioned opposite the school's toilets. Anyway, as grateful as I was for my books, I was able to fit another interest into my socially barren life since Cerys and Garth had left it with an achingly noticeable void.

Like did I know that my developing appreciation of music in the late seventies was to pull me down into the emotional depths in the late eighties, but that is for another chapter.

Eighties Roar

The eighties decade was to turn out to be much more significant for me as my great-aunt, Lyn, retired from work and decided to return to her family home to live with confirmed bachelor, Rhys, who was not pleased with the disruption to his solitude.

My aunt was a tiny woman and I believe that she did not feel safe living by herself anywhere.

My aunt's arrival back to the family fold was a couple of years after the loss of Garth and Cerys, which was a void I filled in by joining my gran in her gardening activities. Gran had devised her own gardening techniques by feeding her lawns with a watering can, filled with beer. The lawn must have loved their unique feed because they soon became greener than usual, and Gran's neighbour could claim, 'the grass was greener on the other side.'

I had Cerys to thank for my love of flowers, and it was the one interest I shared with my outgoing Gran, who had always been a social butterfly. Poor Gran, who must have wondered where her withdrawn and anti-social grandchild came from. I seldom smiled and spoke only when I was spoken to. I had given up bothering with my peers, whose games I couldn't participate in, and who were louder, and more boisterous than me. My aunt was quiet like me, and I admired her for choosing a career over marriage in an era when such a decision took courage. We formed an unlikely bond.

Aunt Lyn living only a mile away in my old village gave me the perfect excuse to visit the little slice of paradise in which my family had grown up. Lyn made me my favourite dish of all: burnt toast, which she almost cremated. Lyn never used margarine as she preferred the farmhouse butter of her youth.

After the burnt toast, I raid Rhys's garden for his peas in the pod, which eaten raw were achingly sweet. The garden's wildlife fascinated me too with its butterflies, bees and ladybirds. I had a curiosity of the natural world which did not extend to human society, even the universe amazed me.

On a summer's late evening, I would take Lyn's powerful field glasses into a back room and inspect the surface of the moon close up. I was disappointed to find it full of disfiguring craters. I guess a normal girl of my age would have been using binoculars to spy on distant neighbours, but I was no normal girl, apart from my interest in cartoons, and a budding interest in comedies such as Allo Allo.

Around this time, I developed a weird obsession with fortune-telling, which was pricked by a visit to a Romany palm reader when I was ten. Lyn had taken me to some festival in mid-Wales celebrating everything Victorian, which included the parking of an authentic wooden, Romany caravan on the town's outskirts.

The palm reading was far from accurate with the woman predicting two future kids for me even though I had known by the age of eight that I was un-maternal. I made this startling discovery during the annual nativity play when I looked upon the Virgin Mary and felt only pity for her. I was mortified when a teacher informed us that she had been visited by an archangel and notified that she was to be impregnated by the Holy Spirit. I felt Mary had no choice in a fate chosen for her with her own Immaculate Conception. Of course, Mary accepted her destiny, but my youthful mind found it all disturbing. I couldn't understand why anyone would want any pregnancy let alone an unplanned one, even one determined by God himself. I am not casting aspersions on Christ's birth; it was just that the circumstances of my own birth were so miserable. My mind had forever linked pregnancy and birth with spousal rejection and my mum's subsequent depression, or—to be more precise—her heartbreak and prolonged grief at the loss of a love, which never was.

My mum's protracted grieving process for her ex taught me a valuable lesson at an early age, which was that love was never what it seemed. In Mum's case, it had always been illusionary; it was an illusion thrown out by a plausible trickster, who had taken her in so completely that she spent the whole of my childhood trying to turn me against him. I would just look at her and think, 'If this is what romantic love does to you then I want nothing to do with it.'

If the reader is wondering why she didn't visit her doctor back then, well, the explanation is simply because there were no anti-depressants available. The medicine for anxiety was limited to Valium or something else equally highly addictive, and even if the depression medicine had been more progressive nobody would admit to being depressed, not even to a trusted G.P. They would use other terminology to inadequately describe their shameful ailment, a disease which dare not speak its name.

Maybe, in being a reluctant witness to my mother's steady mental decline, I had just witnessed the destructive side of love all my life, which in my childlike mind I identified with the mythic figure, Narcissus, in one of my many books. The story of Narcissus and Echo was accompanied by the illustration of a handsome youth gazing at the reflection of himself in a clear pond. The fixation of his self-image was his punishment for spurning the advances of Nymph Echo, who pined away for him until only her voice was left. The moral of the story being that the heartless lad was condemned to be forever fixed emotionally at a certain age without any ability for spiritual growth.

This seemed true of Mum's ex who lacked both a sense of responsibility and empathy. Unfortunately, it was also true of my mother, who lived in the past for a lost lover, and lacked either the ability or willingness to move into the present, which I guess is the curse of overwhelming hatred for a person who is out of her reach, but still very much present in her mind. The git had become like a ghost haunting her life across the decades; he was a Willo-the-Wisp creature in his capacity to lure her into a paralysing swamp from which there was no escape. There was only this static existence which froze her in the sixties and made any emotional mobility impossible. It was no wonder my concept of love became warped after seeing the psychological devastation it caused, not to mention the fact that we were living in economic deprivation because of his selfish refusal to pay maintenance. I had made up my mind at an early age that I would never meet him, but his monstrous shadow was still cast over both of us; after all, it had brought normal life to a grinding halt for my mother, and, as for me, I was far from normal.

Anyway, getting back to my meeting with the traveller, in spite of her less than impressive reading, I still developed a brief obsession with delving into the future. I was hopeful about my future despite the upheavals of the past, or maybe because of a deep desire to move on from the past. However, my scrying into mirrors refused to give away anything of my future.

I soon gave up on my scrying attempts when I discovered a new passion, Wonder Woman with Linda Carter at the age of ten. The character was everything I longed to be: strong, outspoken, tall, athletic and fearless.

Wonder Woman was my first female role model. Yes, I was proud of Aunt Lyn, but my poor aunt was so short that I towered over by the age of ten. Also, Lyn had such a fondness for rich food that she was nearly as wide as she was tall. Neither did Lyn possess Carter's stunning looks, although I was less enamoured by female beauty than I was by female strength which was rarely displayed so blatantly back then, at least, not where I lived.

The women in my family possessed a sort of covert resilience to all the testing rigours of working-class life, but in my childish naivety, I did not realise how tough they were, especially my mother who had to literally fend of predatory men in her bar job.

Compared to Lyn, Gran and my mother, I was fragile and meek, and my timidity, when being confronted by any bully, often caused me to reproach myself, particularly when I was often reduced to tears. I knew they regarded me as weak, and rightly so because I saw myself as weak although I had never been taught to stand up for myself by a mother who was fuelled with a quick spark temper, which in me manifested itself as a festering longing for revenge, which was enacted in my fantasy world. In reality, I seldom answered back against even the meanest comment delivered in the most aggressive tone. I would defend myself during occasional physical fights when I was cornered, which thankfully were rare events.

It was in Lyn's parlour that I watched my idol batter baddies, and it was in her parlour that I continued my private education through her collection of books. Lyn was much more preoccupied with education either Gran or Mum, who had daydreamed in class.

I don't perceive this as laziness because the expectations on working-class women (unless exceptionally bright) were nil in Gran's day, and low in the sixties.

Neither of the women had valued education whilst at school, and I suspect that the only reason Mum had pushed me to read was because she did not want the teachers complaining I was illiterate, which would have given them more ammunition to fire against a single-parent mother. A woman already labelled as a troublemaker, even though they had given up on me in nursery school.

My visits to Lyn—sometimes with Gran—were to teach me a lot about life, since I was able to observe their sibling relationship, which was sometimes comic like the time Gran went hunting for special healing weeds down by the river. When Gran came back, she soaked them in a watery basin into which Lyn placed her swollen feet. Amazingly, thirty minutes later the swelling was considerably removed, and I started to see Gran in a fresh light, as not just a wife and mother, but as a miracle worker capable of building gardens from scratch and healing swollen feet.

I came to understand that herbal knowledge had been

passed down from their mother, and I was thankful for it when, one New Year's Eve, Aunt Lyn made me a concoction of boiling water mixed with whiskey for my cold, which not only worked but was the first time I enjoyed New Year's Eve in my ten years on Earth.

Gran also had medicinal uses for whiskey, which she would mix with vegetable oil ready to rub into her arthritic knees, which had seen too many hard surfaces during their long time working in domestic service.

They were women who were wise in an understated way, which was no longer appreciated in a modern world of science, medication and technological advances. My two cousins living eight miles away already possessed computers and printers, which were a middle-class privilege in the early eighties.

There were no computers in my school, which was so traditional that up to the early eighties we were using wooden desks with inkwells and lids which opened to reveal containers loaded with all kinds of childish delights. Of course, the inkwells were no longer used even though some of us used the fountain pen with cartridges, which were always resting on candy pink blotting paper always stained with blobs of vein coloured ink. There was something classy about using the fountain tip as opposed to a common old biro despite the mess; I personally loved the subtle fragrance of ink, which I found more appealing than sickly smelling perfume. I guess ink reeked of history as did the chalkboards in a way in which modern classes can't.

At the age of ten, I experienced my first holiday, which was a school trip to North Wales, which I went along to because everybody else in the class was going. I only went along because our teacher mentioned the story of a nun's ghost in the communal shower space; it sounded so exciting, and I wanted to catch a glimpse of my first ghost. I had always loved ghost stories, and, suddenly, I had a chance to be in my own ghost adventure. Of course, it didn't enter my head that there was no reason for a phantom nun to haunt a kids' holiday centre. As it turns out, the centre was a long hall with a dozen dormitories attached to it in the middle of a field.

Even though the centre was not far from the beach, we spent most of the week stuck in the field attending Welsh lessons apart from the odd activity such as horse riding and candle making. No wonder our teacher had told that story, which was to spice up a dreary place that was a school from school. I felt cheated and couldn't wait for the week to end.

I was disappointed, especially when my ghost failed to materialise, but worse was to come when I developed the runs mid-week. The runs were so severe that watery faeces poured out of me before I could reach the toilet, and faeces soiled knickers mounted up in my suitcase. There was no way I could rinse them because I would have had to dry them on the dorm's radiator, which I shared with five others. I was not showing the girls my shitty knickers. I kept my suitcase under the bed and each time I opened it, the stench of faeces drenched knickers violated my over-sensitive nose. I imagined it wafting over to the next bed, and then everyone would sniff out my odious secret. I dreaded their reaction since I had already my mother's novel, Carrie, and I had been disturbed by the first chapter's shower scene, which was now flashed back into my mind like some aroused sleeping ghoul whose crypt had been abruptly smashed apart. Instead of having sanitary towels flung at me, the girls would pelt me with my own underwear, and I would be found cowering in a corner with stinking panties hanging over my face. It's funny how certain books have a capacity to seep into your subconscious where they lay dormant waiting for any trigger to thrust them into the front of your consciousness.

I was desperate to leave and bawled every evening, not caring who saw me, or what they thought. I couldn't tell anyone I was covered in my own muck and was relieved that everyone put it down to homesickness. I left there without learning a word of Welsh and, even worse, the nun never put in an appearance. As for my ruined pants, they all had to be binned. That nightmarish holiday should have taught me a lesson about not leaving my over-oiled fantasy life dictate my decisions in reality; it was to be the first ordeal of many because of my inability to make pragmatic choices. Alas, a year later, at the age of eleven, fatuous Brian was about to enter my life, whose influence on Mum's and my own life was to be negative, to say the least. Before the arrival of weird Brian, there was the matter of getting me kitted out in uniform for comprehensive school. My visit to comprehensive school, a year earlier, coincided with Gran and Mum getting cleaning work at my village school.

This was a feat of bravery for Mum, who had bad memories of one particular classroom, which had once contained a coal fire. My mother's desk had been placed in front of the fire, which would blow out towards her every time a strong gust of wind blew down the chimney.

The distracting effect of the lively fireplace stopped my mother from working, and she was kept back a year in the class. My mother was so terrified of the fire that when she re-entered the classroom years after the fireplace had been removed she still swore she could smell whiffs of ancient sulphur raising out of a wall, which had long since been filled in by concrete.

The only positive of that fateful year was my mother joining gingerbread not long after I turned eleven. Gingerbread was a group set up for single-parents, which was based miles out of town since there were still few single-parents in my area even in the eighties.

The main benefit of gingerbread was the cheap holidays, and we managed one to Portsmouth where we stayed in student digs, which Mum and her newfound friend were sharing, who had to clean out before we could use the kitchen.

The woman had two sons about my age, who she would frequently clip across the ear, which sounds harsh but from my experience of Mum slapping my hand, I knew that firstly the women struggled to cope alone, with no one to share problems with. Secondly, a single-parent is forced to play the role of the dad.

This is important because I remember when I was seven watching an American cartoon called, Wait Until Your Father Gets Home, in which a desperate Mum screams at her unruly brats, 'Wait until your father gets home.' The father being the disciplinarian of the home, whilst the Mum is the cookie baking homemaker. It was then it occurred to me that two parents play different roles which not only complement each other but are vital for the raising of healthy kids. I was struck by how much I was missing out by not having a parent around, who would not just play an instrumental role in my upbringing but would also give me a proper concept of masculinity as an authoritarian yet protective force.

I saw my grandad and uncle daily though they were so

exhausted from mining that they would expect Gran to make their tea and me to make their coffee as soon as I was old enough to lift a steel kettle. I didn't mind except that neither spoke to me and only spoke to Gran to bark out orders; it was a macho household in a macho society. The only aspect of masculinity I saw was spoilt and aggressive and looking back, it was giving me a negative view of males in general. Yes, they were breadwinners, yet they were also emotionally remote towards women since they valued the camaraderie of other miners before relationships with wives and daughters.

There were my two elder uncles visiting, who were businessmen and middle-class, so I didn't particularly relate to them either; it was apparent on their visits in their Mercedes or posh cars that they lived in a world of greater comfort, education with their computers and more expansive travel. Their expectations in life were rightly greater than that of their working-class relatives, who expected nothing and got nothing. There was a sense of entitlement with them and my cousins, which was absent in the blue-collar folk. Don't get me wrong because I am not faulting their high expectations in life as it seemed to work for them. Maybe it was what drove their motivation to succeed. However, because of my fractured self-confidence, I couldn't imagine any success and never expected to live in their world. There was no real role model I could emulate, thus I ended up envying kids with two parents, especially affluent parents.

Anyway, I ramble on too much, and getting back to Portsmouth it was a nice break, despite the ear boxing. We had fun one day, thanks to my mother's verbal clangers. We had got on a bus somewhere in Portsmouth and Mum informed the bus driver, 'We want to go to the centre of

Bournemouth!'

The bus driver cast a wary eye at the ditz before him and replied, 'Get on and get off where you want!'

We had a free bus ride that day because neither Mum nor her mate knew where they wanted to go, but God knows what the poor driver thought of us. Mum was always opening her gob without thinking, which I was doing occasionally in the class. My ill-conceived comments were attracting much derision, so I ended up developing selective mutism, which might have protected me from ridicule, though it was creating contempt for my unwillingness to communicate. I ended up feeling that whether I opened my beak or not, I couldn't starve off the bullies. Bizarrely, I preferred contempt to mockery since I could bear being seen as rude but not foolish. I already felt stupid because of my inability to mingle and mocking laughter confirmed this.

The laughter rose up in front of me and bounced off all the class walls like some monstrous Echo, which was invisible yet still able to make its presence felt as it travelled from one end of the room to another feeding off my potent insecurity and shame with the lust of a vampire.

Little did I realise that school bullies were to be the least of my problems with the unwelcome arrival of Brian, which was to adversely change both our lives. Brian was one of the barflies where Mum worked on the weekends; he was unhappily married to a husband beater. Mum had only known him a few months when Brian decided to suddenly leave his wife and two teenage kids for her one night.

Brian had apparently endured a final beating without fighting back even though he was six foot and nearly obese. I instantly disrespected him for that since I had always fought

43

back against physical bullies even ones bigger than me, and I was a timid child. The men in my family apart from Rhys were all tough fighters, and none of them would have allowed themselves to be pushed around by any woman; I don't even recall Gran raising her voice to Grandad ever, even when he sat in front of the TV watching her pour coal on the fire. Gran had to clean out mucky ash from the fire's metallic bowels in which the remains of digested coal clinkers had been laid to rest. Brian was also greedy, and everything he ate was layered with fat, even his lava bread—this is boiled seaweed, which was healthy until Brian fried it with bacon fat—although his favourite red meat was fried pork guzzled with fried chips. In fact, Brian fried everything. The problem with this was that when he moved in with us, he took over the cooking role from Mum, which had been plain but fat-free food, and replaced it with fat loaded pork, chips, crackers and full-fat mature cheese. I have got to say at this point in the narrative that I was a child who loved my food (providing it was either savoury or chocolate), but I was used to wholesome food, and I was alarmed to see Mum piling on the pounds as soon as Brian moved in. Thankfully, I never put on weight in spite of Brian's cooking, and the crackers and cheese I acquired a taste for, which Brian bought in bulk. I found out years later that Brian had grown up in a household loaded with food, which had taken priority over clothes. This was not unusual in Wales years ago when the main mission of a mum would be to feed up a child in the belief that a chubby child was a bonny child, and my gran knew of one mother who would fry chips for her brood in butter. The only benefit to Brian's love of fat drenched food was that he would come home from work on building sites daily at four and stay in the kitchen until five, which gave me the TV all to myself to watch my favourite cartoon, He-Man, King of the Universe. For those unfamiliar with He-Man and his nemesis, Skeletor; he was a blonde, athletic hero fighting arch-villain, Skeletor, whose skull features were in sharp contrast to those of attractive He-Man.

However, I never watched it to see the baddie defeated because I wrongly perceived Skeletor as somehow misunderstood in his friendless world; I even identified with lonely Skeletor, which was a pretty warped way of thinking. My mother had once pointed out to me an article which claimed that loners were more likely to kill than the socially adjusted, and as for me, I was socially maladjusted. I went totally along with this since I was already killing bullies in my fantasies. Maybe it was only a matter of time before fantasy spilt out into reality.

Whatever the truth of the article, I had always rooted for the anti-hero, not because of their anti-social tendencies but because they could only operate from the margins of a society that had shunned them. After all, I lived on society's outskirts because of my unfriendliness so maybe I was no better from them. Maybe they had started life similar to me, different for some reason—as was the case with Skeletor—and things had slid downwards from there.

My life was certainly on a downward slide because Brian was bringing more inward resentment into it; it wasn't just his vile food. There was something not right about the guy; he was always trying to frighten me with childish faces and a zombie walk, which was just irritating. Worse of all, he hollered down anyone in disagreement, which would be yells peppered with curses including his favourites, 'bitch' and 'bastard', which according to Mum was the way his mother spoke.

My mother hated the usage of the word 'bitch' which the men in her family never uttered despite being miners in a sexist culture where machismo reigned supreme. However, there was still a sense of chivalry, which had given rise to the working men's clubs in which the men were separated from the women by their own men's room. One of the purposes of these rooms was to give men space to use language that might offend womenfolk, who were confined off in a smaller room; it was for men to let off copious amounts of verbal steam without any 'ladies' present, except, of course, the barmaid, who didn't count.

Brian seemed to consider most women 'bitches', and I am sure it was linked to his phobia of witches. Why Brian had a fear of witches, I will never know, but when a family friend told Mum that his mother had spoilt Brian, it sort of made sense. Brian was certainly immature, and if his maternal influence was a harsh woman who had spoiled him to the detriment of his sister then Brian's perception of women must certainly have been twisted.

I never met the woman since my mother—who detested her—forbade me to visit her and avoided visiting the woman herself as much as was possible, but it was still evident, even to me, that Brian was in an arrested state of emotional development, which seemed to have grinded to a shuddering halt when he was a teenager. It explained his toilet, rude sense of humour, which attempted to sexualise innocent words, in fact, Brian could sexualise anything in his gutter like mind; he certainly had sex constantly on his brain, or what passed for one.

Brian, like most folk of his generation in Wales, had left

school at fifteen to pursue manual labour, which in men's cases would have been mining, farm labouring, building or factory work, whereas women would have been left with factories, cleaning, or bar work; hairdressing, if they were lucky enough to have parents who could afford the course. Therefore Brian's lack of education partially excused his limited communication skills and general ignorance, but it didn't excuse his lack of basic social skills such as the total lack of empathy he often displayed whilst being obnoxious. In fact, Brian had a total disregard for the feeling of others.

I lacked empathy but I had difficulty reading facial expressions and body language, although in Brian's case I suspected that it was more than this. After all, he had left his two kids without further contact with them and using his fear of his wife as an excuse. In retrospect (apart from being charmless), he displayed many of Mum's ex's traits: irresponsibility, fecklessness, insensitivity and even outright callousness. In short, he was never going to be the paternal role model I needed or the caring partner Mum desperately needed. I even came to resent his rich food, which oozed out his negativity and longed for my mother's plain dishes even though the dry mash was layered with undissolved powder.

I can't imagine what it was like for Mum to end up with another selfish creep though. At least, I sort of had my grandad as a model of a proper man, and as aloof as he, I admired his resilience and stamina in the face of two bouts of pleurisy, which were work-related, whereas Mum had some weak creature, who had been terrorised by a small woman. There was obviously a pattern emerging in poor Mum's love life, which I am convinced had been caused by her sheltered upbringing.

The miners' strike soon took my mind off Brian, which lasted a year, and ended the family tradition for my grandad and youngest uncle, although we still carried on using coal fires from open cast coal mines in the area. Miners, including Grandad, managed to find work in local factories. I didn't bemoan the end of the deep mines loaded with their cargo of black diamonds. It had been an unhealthy even dangerous work with tales of men getting trapped in mine shafts overnight and being found in the morning, insane. By this time, I had moved onto twelve and was looking forward to my first holiday abroad in Benidorm. It was here that I was to make a startling discovery about Brian. It was one day whilst we were out shopping that the three of us entered a Chinese owned gift store. Brian and I waited for my mother outside for what seemed a long time. Eventually, Brian warily ventured in as though entering some dragon's den. He soon came out ashen-faced.

'She's gone!'

'She can't be.' I reasoned.

Brian came to a crazy conclusion, 'They've kidnapped her!'

'What?'

'The Chinese owners have taken her for the white slave trade!' Brian's voice was full of panic.

Even I knew this was unlikely since Mum was way too old to be trafficked and trying not to laugh at his idiocy, I suggested, 'Go back in and ask the owner where she is.'

There was no way coward Brian was going back in, and he raced to our hotel leaving me sniggering behind him. I should have been crying at his mix of cowardice and racial discrimination. There were Asians in our nearest town, and none of them was linked to white slavery; they all did honest work. Besides, the notion that a store owner was abducting his customers was too ridiculous for words. I was starting to see Brian as a racist idiot, and when it turned out that Mum was at the hotel after leaving through a back door, well Brian looked even sillier. We all had a good laugh at this incident, but we should have been alarmed at a total lack of common sense from a person I already disrespected.

Back to school and I managed to make one friend, who was closer to her middle-class mates, and I only stuck with her because I was fast being labelled as the school loner. All the girls in my class were middle-class and went clothes shopping every Saturday with their pocket money, whereas I was forced to get by on school meals, which meant I couldn't join them at the chippie every afternoon. In a way, it suited me because I had nothing in common with them; I couldn't even pretend to be confident in my old-fashioned shoes and coat. There was no way I could ask Mum for a clothes allowance knowing she struggled to buy me birthday clothes, besides, I was lucky to have a wardrobe in my room. My mum had shared a damp, ant-infested bedroom with two brothers, which had been too small for any furniture, so Gran had just piled their clothes on their beds where ants slumbered under pillows. In the morning, ironed bundles of clothes peppered the floor.

As for Brian, he dressed in rags after spending all his money on buying cupboards full of food as if he was preparing for some future famine.

Brian had some food obsession which was excessive even to a foodie such as myself. It occurred to me that there was no balance in the guy's life because everything was done to excess: eating, smoking and drinking. The trouble was there was no balance in my life either, because my mother had been weakened by her ex, and Brian was just feeble. There was no one I could really look up to, or even go to for any advice such as dealing with the bullies. My mother had battered bullies in school, but I was forced to ignore verbal sparring since I had no wit to adequately reply to sarcasm and jokes at my expense. The bullies had already taken my self-imposed silence as an indicator of stupidity, and my only release from it all was my books, which by now were adult novels and Saturday morning chart shows.

Around this age, I started to suffer from stomach cramps, which always came on shortly after lunch, and gradually became so agonising by the end of the school day that I would be getting off the bus doubled in pain. Since the cramps eased off leaving school I was left in doubt that the pain was being caused by a build-up of suppressed tension, which was twisting my guts into a bundle of tight knots. It was like strings on a violin being pulled so forcefully that it was only a matter of time before they snapped with a barely audible whimper; it was pathetic and I knew it. The trouble was I didn't know what to do about it.

My mother had tried various doctors to find out what was up with her increasingly withdrawn child, who spent all her spare time shut away in the bedroom. I never discussed my problems with her because she was incapable of solving her own, and I had learned from an early age that I was on my own when it came to any school issues because both she and Gran made references to my unsociability and were obviously despairing of an unsmiling, unfriendly child. I suppose from their point of view, my unpopularity with my peers was letting the family down even though it was a dysfunctional family with all things taken into account, least of all the strange conduct of Brian who had taken to avoiding neighbours in the garden. This was not rudeness on his part because anyone who knew him was aware that his only conversation was smut laced with obscene language. We were glad that the neighbours never got a chance to speak to him because they would have pitied poor Mum.

At the age of thirteen, my first pet dog came into my life, which Gran had rescued from a dog's kennel; it was an old spaniel dog, which had once belonged to my mother's needlework teacher. The teacher had hated Mum, who daydreamed throughout her class, and it seemed a strange turn of events that we ended up with the deceased woman's dog.

I was given the duty of walking the dog after school, which got me away from the foul-mouthed rants of Brian and a screaming match if my mother told him to shut up. Any attempts to silence Brian were met with manipulation tactics such as: 'What's wrong with you? You're in a mood!' My mother soon gave up attempts to gag him. Brian would never take responsibility for any appalling behaviour, and he never apologised for anything. Why would he? He was never in the wrong. In spite of his lack of intellect, he managed to convince us that we were wrong for reproaching him; it amazed me that such a dull bloke could be so cunning. There was nothing we could do because there was no such thing then as emotional abuse, and even marital rape was still legal in the mid-eighties.

The one plus to the mid-eighties was the introduction of S4C or Welsh language TV, which was the Welsh alternative to channel 4, which had been introduced in England a few years earlier. Wales was not to gain access to channel four (unless you were a Sky customer) until the introduction of digital TV. My Aunt Lyn loved S4C, but non-Welsh speakers like Mum were annoyed that we could not get the benefits of four English speaking channels. But S4C went a long way to bringing back Welsh from the brink of extinction.

Just before my fourteenth birthday, I took a school trip to Germany with my so-called mate who was better than no mate at all (just). On the second day of the stay, I woke up to find blood draining out of me. The cluster of acne erupting onto my cheeks ought to have warned me of impending menarche, and once again, I experienced the panic, which had beset me in North Wales. This time the mounting panic was compounded by all the implications of menarche, not least unwanted fertility.

However, for me, it had always been highly symbolic of the Biblical Fall; I had read the Genesis story in a children's Bible five years earlier. Eve's rejection by God and the subsequent expulsion from Eden was a punishment for her loss of innocence and temptation of Adam. Poor Eve also got the 'curse' of menstruation, which accompanied her fall from God's Grace. Understandably, my view of puberty was negative and represented the possibility of unwanted maternity and its responsibilities. It was a day I dreaded anyway as I saw my corseted childhood ebb away, and for it to occur in a foreign country where there was no sign of any chemist, and I was unable to ask for directions in German was terrifying.

I was too ashamed to ask a teacher for sanitary towels; I was reduced to stuffing my pants with reams of toilet paper, which did not altogether stem the blood flow. Inevitably all my trousers were stained, and once again, I was faced with a suitcase full of soiled clothes; it looked like history was repeating itself on another school trip. Once again, I was mortified into shocked silence, only this time my mortification was to be permanent because adolescence had found me; it was making its vile presence felt, and life was to change for the worse, much worse.

Menarche heralded a long period of depression for me as surely as a dead canary down the mine is an indication of methane gas. This is a dramatic comparison to make, but my slide into utter gloom was inevitable, even before my face became pus infested, and my hair always shining with grease despite a daily wash, all this being more fodder for bullies on top of my absence of self-esteem.

I had coped with being an outcast before because I had lived in a future realm beyond school, which was an adult world free of taunts, but any sufferer of depression will tell you that the illness forces the sufferer to live from day to day in the present since the future is a long stretch of hopelessness. In fact, you can't even see the future as it is once a mass of dense fog waiting to wrap its grey tentacles of despair around you. Yes, it is safe to say I lost what little joy was left to me in simple pleasures such as the dog's walks, music and even my books, which sat on my shelf silently reproaching me. Not only did I lose my love of music, but the thought of all my favourite singers leading glamorous lives whilst I rotted away in a cul-de-sac boil bashing my putrid face made my mental malaise all the more distressing. It just wasn't fair that they were being adored worldwide whereas I faced a daily barrage of verbal vitriol, a sad mother and her boyfriend, who could only be described as an unfunny clown. Their talent and beauty highlighted my own sense of unworthiness. I was like the uninvited witch in Sleeping Beauty, who was shunned by the beautiful.

I don't think it was any coincidence that the fog pounced during the onset of my turbulent adolescence. I was emotionally unprepared for menstruation anyway, but adulthood looking like a walking oil slick was almost unbearable. I had been a bonny child, and the transition into a gross woman was not what I envisioned. The only relief was that my figure remained scrawny, even infantile without obvious curves. Yes, I was an odd teenager, whose deepest desires flew in the face of what ought to have been an exciting process from childhood to adulthood.

If I hadn't been such a compulsive eater in possession of a gob which could demolish a plate load of food faster than rampaging locusts I would have been anorexic. I became fascinated with self-starvation. My mum's mate was anorexic, and I admired her steely discipline and girlish figure even when her fingers locked into a frozen position, one day, as a result of years without nutrition. I completely got anorexia (which was then misunderstood as dieting) as a means of controlling the one thing in life a disempowered woman could control: her body. Well both my life and body were out of my control as I desperately scrubbed away at the pustules and hid all signs of streaming blood with *discreet* tampons. Discretion being the buzz word of tampon adverts in the eighties as women got manipulated by a sales pitch making a profit from our horror of being caught bleeding.

A small respite from my misery came at sixteen when I decided to leave, in 1989, for college. I can't say I was going to miss the eighties with its stupid power dressing inspired by

Dynasty, and apart from rockers, like Guns and Roses, the music had gone soft in the era of the Romantics. The Yuppies had replaced the extinct miners with their motto of 'greed is good'. Roll on the nineties. I was once more looking towards a hopeful future, which immediately pushed the fog into the background. Notice my usage of the word 'background' as opposed to pushed away because the truth is this: my depression was not vanquished; it had made a temporary retreat into the distance as it prepared for the next battle in our ongoing war. In other words, it was lulling me into a false sense of security. To utilise modern terminology, fake security.

Nineties Hope and Madness

I left school without qualifications since protracted depression had extinguished all my concentration, which meant that my college course was going to be a Mickey Mouse type beauty course, which covered manicures, pedicures and facials. It meant weekday stays in mid-Wales and weekends at home, which was fine with me since every Saturday night after leaving pubs, Brian and Mum were having slanging matches over his womanising.

The town was a white reflection of my home town with just one Asian family (the same as my home town). Whereas my home town had one black lad in the entire junior school, and white girl in our entire comprehensive school, this town seemed entirely devoid of black folk. However, its lack of diversity could be explained by its lack of industry and social deprivation, which was a consequence of its rural location. That said, there was an equal amount of English folk in the town as Welsh, and even the odd Romany traveller could be found there.

I had not chosen the course with any particular career in mind; I had gone for it to slap on make-up daily and prove the bullies wrong or at least wrong about me being ugly. In hindsight, I had really not thought out the practicalities of my decision, which meant I was making the first shambolic life-choice of many in my ridiculous life.

Although my fog had billowed away into the sunset, the systematic bullying I had endured since eleven had eroded away all my confidence, which made me so cripplingly shy that making friends was going to be difficult especially with all of the narcissistic type girls who mainly populated the course.

The main salon was a narcissistic paradise with its wall-length mirror in which all the girls daily preened themselves, which soon became a bizarre kind of ritual for us. No one there could pass the mirror without resisting a quick peek at their overtly made-up faces, which would not have looked out of place in a circus. The make-up was enforced by even make garishly done lecturers, who were as shallow as their students.

Anyway, you will recall my scrying obsession in chapter one as a means of communication with the future, but I had ignored other mysteries surrounding mirrors as a child such as myths about the looking glass entrapping water sprites. The water spirits got their revenge by causing trouble for whoever was reflected in the mirror. Suddenly, when faced with a mirror of epic proportion, a warning bell rung out in my head telling me that this was not good. Smashing every mirror in the room and risking a lifetime jink would have been better than gazing at a face so creamed and powered that it seemed to belong to someone else who had stolen my identity, ready to destroy me.

Some of the mirror gazers stayed in my bedsit, and the ones from middle-class backgrounds were so different to me in their effortless social ease, but I also figured that they enjoyed the benefits of proper parenting. When I say this, I am not criticising my mother; she had been abandoned by her ex during the most pivotal moment of her life, then got stuck with a geezer who was socially inadequate, even worse unsupportive. Brian was a more uncouth version of her ex.

Even the working-class girls on my course were possessed of a self-belief that I lacked! At the time, I had put their extreme self-obsessed personalities down to their lack of maturity since most of them were school leavers. Once again, I became a loner spending my break times in the college library and my lunchtimes in a leafy park, whose central feature was an elongated waterfall. I could spend all day gazing at the cascading water, which had a rejuvenating effect on my defeated spirit. Even being on a glamorous course didn't change my low opinion of myself.

It was by accident I met my first boyfriend, who my immature mind regarded as a saviour. The eighteen-year-old lad, Carl (who was doing a business course), was plain, short even physically unattractive but radiated a self-assured, cheeky charm which attracted me. Crucially, Carl had been raised by a gracious businesswoman. Little did I know that Carl had been irreversibly damaged by an upbringing more disturbing than mine, yet I was not to find this out until years later. Whatever deep-rooted insecurities plagued him, they were carefully concealed by a veneer of assurance that bordered on arrogance. The conceit appealed to me because I was fascinated by any person outgoing and socially assured, the opposite of my social anxiety. The truth was I was stunningly naive, even dangerously so, and his brazenness should have been a red alert, though back then I was lapping up his jovial attention which would now be recognised as *love bombing.*

Now the reader will be aware that in a previous chapter, I mentioned love as an alien concept to me. Yes, I loved my dog, but as far anything romantic was concerned my heart was firmly bolted with a padlock swinging from the end of the bolt. This sounds saddening but actually, my inability to fall in love was going to serve me well in a relationship which was becoming verbally abusive, as Carl soon pounced on any weakness I stupidly revealed. I was still too trusting after years of only seeing the dark side of my peers, but I am thankful that I never fell for him. I was just enjoying being around someone who was everything I was not. Best of all, he had rescued me (briefly) from a year of loneliness and weight baiting from classmates who were envious of my slender frame such is the petulance of narcissism.

My only friend at that time was a neighbour, at the bottom of my street, who I got friendly with by chance one Saturday. Ceri was sunning herself out in her garden as I walked past her place during a dog walk. As my dog sniffed about at the base of her wall, Ceri came over to stroke him. Ceri was in her forties, divorced and with a twenty-year-old daughter, but somehow we struck up a friendship. We had nothing in common except that Ceri was a kind lady, who accepted me in a way in which I had not felt accepted since the loss of Garth and Cerys. I guess Ceri was as lonely as I was since her daughter was out most evening partying. Ceri turned out to be a fascinating lady, who, one Easter, showed me her Stigmata wounds on her feet. Ceri never went to Church, although she was a firm believer in God. When I saw the Stigmata injuries on her feet, I was impressed even though I was no Christian; I was so angry with God for all the blows I had been dealt in life that I concluded that if there was a higher power than it was punishing my mother and me for reasons unknown. I tried not to think of Spirit too much because I would always recall a teacher in our school assembly making the Biblical quote, "God works in mysterious ways," which for me was a cop-out way of saying that shit happens to folk who didn't deserve it. Folk like my family who had innocently gone about their lives in their idyllic village before the idyll was permanently shattered by the arrival of Mum's ex. I regret this thinking now because, really, my family were too idealistic in their outlook without awareness of cruel reality. I am certain that part of the problem was being in an isolated village corseted by a wall of conjoined mountains, all of which so effortlessly flowed into each other that I couldn't tell where one mountain ended and the other began.

Mountains do funny things to the valley psyche both positive and negative depending on where you are positioned. When I was walking the dog to a mountain's peak, I was given a sort of godly perspective on the community below, which sounds somewhat egotistic, but this supreme view beats spending too much time at the mountains' base. Although the mountains have the benefit of making one feel secure in their rugged embrace, there is the disadvantage of feeling physically and mentally restrained by their very presence. Almost as though they are drifting towards you, and gradually encroaching on your limited space until you are morally crushed. I always wondered what would happen to valley folk if a giant hand knocked down the mountains leaving us with open space. Would the valley dwellers become less petty? Less neighbour obsessed? Less able to bear lifelong grudges with a fervent zeal? Less demanding of frivolous gossip? If we had been less sheltered by them, less ingenious, more worldly maybe a conman would have been less able to prey on Mum's affections. It sounds daft to blame the landscape for the problems that besieged valley folk, yet sometimes I couldn't help but see us as captives of the mountains without any awareness of our psychological captivity.

This critique never applied to Ceri, who had escaped the curse of pettiness and spite. Despite our differing views on religion, I was soon visiting Ceri and her daughter, Beth, every weekend. I even got so friendly with them over time that I was spending Friday evenings with Beth and her mates in our local in spite of a ten year age gap between Beth and myself.

As my social life took off, back home, it took only a few months of my non-relationship with Carl to disintegrate into a lack of respect on both sides as I came to realise that Carl was a compulsive liar. Carl must have been laughing at me for months as I lapped up every implausible story until he finally came out with whooper, which challenged even my gullibility. Of course, I would lie to my own family to avoid trouble, but Carl's lying reminded me of the skyscraper tall tales, an attention-seeking girl in my school class used to come up with. I had loathed that girl, who had been a sadistic bully pouncing on every flaw, and here I was going out with one.

Luckily, for me, Carl was getting tired of my possessive behaviour and dumped me on the way to the college in a public place where anyone could have overheard his cold parting shot.

I was secretly relieved, and this act of cowardice demonstrated an irresponsibility which stopped me in my track. I even wondered if his standoffish attitude that week had been deliberately created in order to get me to dump him first, which was exactly what my mother's ex had done to her before their separation. It occurred to me that I had been going out with a charmer seemingly without empathy, a sense of responsibility and possibly without remorse. In other words, I had been dating a replica of my father. Like my mother, I had been taken in without a flicker of suspicion, but unlike her, I had left my heart impenetrably closed.

The only explanation for this is that Carl had sized me up on our first meeting; he had seen someone reserved, friendless and isolated, who he could easily manipulate with his pathetic lies. Sadly, he had also been attracted to my lack of self-esteem, which was attracting every bully on the course. Carl had no respect for me; I had no respect for him; I had no self-respect. He had done me a favour because between his compulsive lying and my compulsive eating/binge drinking we would have been a match made in Dante's Inferno. Why is hell described in such terms? The problem I always encountered with evil was not a raging heat, to the contrary, the problem is a glacial lack of empathy. I grew up without empathy but I was beginning to understand that others felt differently to me; I was learning empathy through my social blunders, whereas narcissists perceive of it as a weakness, which makes them altogether different to the socially incompetent. However, any empathy I gained was hard-won as it became clear to me that I was not meant to get any advantage in life easily. I even had to learn mistrust the tough way because my judgement of others was impaired by non-existent people reading skills. Shortly after, my Friday evenings with Beth were about to end, which was a social disaster I brought on myself. I would drink myself into a near stupor in order to gain a small measure of Dutch courage, or what I would refer to as *wine courage*. I was becoming a binge drinker at sixteen just to mask my social anxieties. I had nothing in common with anyone, not even my own peer group, who would gossip about folk I had no interest in. I didn't seem to fit into any crowd even Beth's group who were all local and working class.

I couldn't even stand up for myself if someone made the meanest comment because I would believe that any unjust criticism was true. I was still back in school only now I was able to gain temporary relief from my fears through an over-indulgence in wine or lager. I was becoming a loose cannon whilst drunk, and Beth rightly finished my Friday jaunts to the pub, though I still kept in contact with her and Ceri on the weekends. Alas, my drinking days were far from over, but for a few years at least Beth had saved me from self-destruction. At the time, I didn't see it this way because the only alcoholic I knew was an old school teacher my mother knew through her bar job; she had been informed that he would knock back fifteen beers at lunchtime before heading back to our school. I was nothing like him I thought since the dangers of weekend binge drinking were not known about then. Of course, the demon drink never leaves you altogether, rather it is lurking around the nearest corner passively waiting.

By this time, Beth and Ceri had become friends with my mother, who had to walk the dog while I was in college. Every time Ceri saw the dog going passed, she made a fuss of him and asked after me; it is amazing how pets can bring folk together. Ceri and Mum had much in common since both were divorced though Ceri's ex had at least stuck around long enough to see Beth grow up. They were no longer the only divorcees in the area, which was becoming increasingly less conservative on issues such as marriage and single mothers since the seventies. The moral stuffiness which had pervaded the valley pre-eighties was gradually, but surely, being eroded as the chapel's grip on the place loosened (it was mainly Lyn's generation attending chapel in this decade).

As life looked up for Mum, I was coming under increasing fire from narcissist bullies on my course. I had even been forced to leave my bedsit because of the hostile atmosphere I sensed there. I understood that it was due to my *aloof manner* as Mum liked to refer to my shyness, but I was sick of being misunderstood because of something beyond my control, which was controlling me. Even if I hadn't felt intimidated by a boisterous crowd, I still didn't feel interesting or witty enough to engage properly with others.

I had not managed to make one friend in the town, and besides, I had gone there without any proper career direction. Even I could see that it was time to leave. I looked into another college course in a town nearer to my own. I gave all my cosmetics to Beth because they had come to represent a part of my life in which I had tried to be something I wasn't; I was never again to wear make-up in the day. Make-up had been a mask, which hadn't enabled me to blend in with more confidence and glamour. In fact, ironically, instead of making me more self-possessed, it had actually robbed me of a proper identity. So much so that when I was advised by a classmate, 'Be yourself', I didn't know what that was. My version of self was as others seemed to see me: timid, shy, awkward and even unapproachable, this was not what I wanted to be or seen to be. The next chapter in my life swung to the opposite direction because up to this point in my seventeen years there had been an imbalance in favour of the feminine, both in my matriarchal family and then in a female-dominated college year. Maybe my deliberate choosing of a male-dominated electronics course was trying to readdress the imbalance, but in the wrong way as my mental pendulum once again swung to another extreme. My off-balance pendulum (as I refer to my instincts) was to do this for the rest of my life as I struggled to find a 'middle way' as the Buddha once accurately summed up the need for moderation in spiritual lives. By now, the reader will be aware that I was anything but moderate in anything I did. If I hadn't had Brian stocking up on tempting food, I would have been anorexic before twenty.

It was the early nineties and an economic recession was hitting the British economy hard with the uncompromising base of Guns and Roses and Aerosmith's music to reflect the economic climate. The Tories were still in administration, but Thatcher had lost her crown along with much of her popularity in former mining communities in which the miners' strike had hit harder than any recession as picking families were forced to rely on collections from neighbours and friends just to feed their families. The recession proved to be nothing as bad as this definitive moment in the community's history despite all the fear-mongering.

In spite of being surrounded by lacklustre menfolk in the family, I chose a vastly different course in electronics, which once again I had chosen after letting my fantasy world dictate my vocational paths in my absurd life. To be fair, to my younger self, I had been confused by my gender since puberty, seeing myself as neither woman nor man. At best, I was a girl such was my arrested emotional development, so with this in mind, it was hardly surprising that I ended up in a class full of males all of whom were white and working-class in a predominantly white town. Diversity in south Wales, back then, was a volatile mix of Welsh, English, Irish, Spanish and Italian post-war migrants. The Spanish and Italian migrants didn't settle into the valleys straight away partly because of a language barrier and partly because they settled into culturally homogeneous regions where outsiders were scant.

Anyway, surprisingly, I got on well with all the lads on my course, who showed no animosity towards the sole female on a testosterone-fuelled course largely due to male lecturers who always went out of their way to make me comfortable. My first three months there, I was truly happy for the first time since the loss of my mates: Cerys and Garth. I even managed to find a nearby park in which to spend my lunchtimes in a self-imposed solitary enclosure. Yes, I was still reclusive, but this time it felt positive without the misunderstandings of easily offended narcissists. In simple terms, I felt accepted for what I was without being made to feel shame over my social inhibitions. All the lads I saw as mates, and none tried to proposition me or act predatory in any way, which was surprising in an all-male group.

Another thing that struck me about the lads was their lack of competitiveness, which had been so obvious in the all-female make-up course with their bitchy antics especially over my weight. Then you got the attractive girls befriending the less attractive ones on the course, which was even more sickening than any vicious comment. I had never been competitive anyway because I was an only child, and I was just too laid back to care what others had. I admired beauty without any envy, which meant that I seldom got jealous, but it also meant that I had no awareness of how destructive this trait is until I went on the beauty course. After a year of bitchiness, it was comforting to be in a less toxic environment. Most of the lads got on with each other and created a co-operative atmosphere, which I guess you could call camaraderie.

I was only there a few months but every day was so positive that it led to my ten minutes of what I now refer to as my 'enlightenment moment' which I label as such for want of a better definition, not to make any misleading comparisons with the Buddha archetype. The moment happened one afternoon after another happy day. As I walked towards my park—which as usual I had all to myself like my own private garden—I felt my brain surge with an inexplicable joy, which bordered on euphoria. By the time, I arrived in the park's centre, I was only able to focus on the sky above. I saw beyond the clouds to the universe which I was aware of instinctively; I sensed its eternal presence dwarfing the planet. Eternity was stretching out before me in all its awesome glory. I basked in a moment that was unearthly and beyond any proper description because I was using the intuitive side of myself which no logic can explain.

I then made the fateful decision to leave, and outside the park, normal thought processes were resumed. As I made my way towards the bus stop, I stopped at a greengrocer to buy— of all things—a pomegranate. I didn't know it at the time but this fruit is highly symbolic in the Christian faith. Painters even depicted the infant Christ with a pomegranate in his hand as an indicator of the suffering which lay ahead in his adult life. If I had been aware of the fruit's association with suffering, I would have gone back to the park, which in its circular construction resembled an Asian mandala. For those unfamiliar with Oriental mandalas, they are essentially a sacred space usually within a circle, sometimes within the confines of a walled space. The closest we get to this religious symbolism in the West is the image of Eden in Genesis, and I wish I had remembered the story at the time.

I am not making any parallels between either Eve's predicament or the saviour Christ's pain with my own bad judgement on this fateful day; it is possible that the pomegranate was just a strange coincidence. If there was any agony in store for me, it was to be largely self-inflicted through bad choices. There sure was a lot of suffering ahead for me, not of the holy, saviour kind, but of the soul-destroying type. I should have stayed in the mandala, yet in my spiritual ignorance, I had no understanding of symbolism neither Western nor Eastern. I was like a blind woman blundering about in the paradise before rejecting some higher power or higher self by leaving a blessed arena.

A couple of weeks later, I was forced to admit that my pathetic maths was making it impossible to stay on a course which was ninety per cent maths. I decided I was done with further education. I was glad for my moment in the park, but I was making foolish choices because of my complete lack of pragmatism. I needed to get into the real world as I raced towards eighteen with nothing to show for it but a few silly mistakes, which would have been avoidable if I had thought clearly.

I did penance for my stupidity by doing various dead-end factory jobs, one of which involved packaging tampons into little, blue boxes (discreet boxes that go unnoticed in one's purse). I willingly paid for my rejection of the divine because for once in my life, I felt it was my fault. If I had been tormented by bullies and mental illness before it was because of something about me which was making me different, and I had no idea if this difference was down to my dysfunctional upbringing, or whether there was something more fundamentally wrong with me. If my problems were due to nature then it was something which could not be labelled because not even all the doctors I had seen over the years knew what it was. Folk in the Orient and Occident talk about karma whatever their faith, but I never felt that my experiences were the result of sins. Up until the day I rejected divinity, I felt I was being made to pay for my father's fecklessness, my mother's inability to cope and fate lumbering me with Brian, a bloke so socially awkward he even made me look like a party animal! It was the first time in my life I felt I deserved any punishment which came my way, which I accepted without resentment.

Well, I soon ran into trouble on the carousel as it spun around leaving me behind. I was the slowest in the factory and got sacked on medical grounds, which was a pattern to be repeated in other factory jobs. In all factories, I was working in all-female groups. Even I could see that there was an imbalance being repeated in my life whether I was in a male-dominated environment or 'bitch group' as I came to call the female populated environments. I don't know whether I was attracting this imbalance towards me, or whether it was a fluke—one thing was for sure—I needed to progress mentally in a mixed group. I needed to get back to college as a mature (twenty-year-old) student, which I could achieve through an access course. There was a place available for me in Newport, which covered subjects such as history, women's studies and languages.

Newport was a small city, though big enough to be free of the relentless gossiping you encounter everywhere in a village. I was glad to be getting away from all that for a year even if it meant long travel every weekend, and relying on my disability payments, which had been rewarded to me because of my newly diagnosed dyspraxia, which had made me unfit for factory work. I was glad for the diagnosis but deeply resentful that it hadn't been diagnosed in school when I was struggling to write figures requiring fine motor skills, not to mention making me useless at all ball games. All those times when I had felt stupid could have been easily avoided if my condition had been given a proper label because dismissive doctors (all-male, middle-class and British) never listened to me, and even laughed when I spoke of my problems. Maybe Mum should have learned her lesson when she had nearly lost a limb because of their incompetence. However, Mum had been raised to show them deference without ever challenging the blatant smugness of some of them. Maybe if her upbringing had instilled more confidence within her, she would have been more rebellious, but I guess generations of being servile to authority made that impossible. Many of our problems were stemming from a lack of esteem, and I was determined to correct this before any more of my lacklustre life got wasted by a lack of self-belief.

I got on well on the course and even managed to make a few good friends with like-minded folk, some of whom had endured deprived backgrounds and all of whom were working-class and burdened with humility much like my own over-zealous modesty. All of us deserved better in life, and all were determined to get it.

At the end of the year, I managed to get a university place in mid-Wales doing a humanities course, which covered multiple and differing courses such as philosophy, psychology, literature, languages, history and artistic subjects. It was a former mining town with rows and rows of terraced homes all huddled together like a line of decaying teeth, you had the feeling that if one was plucked away all the others would fall apart in protest. It was only their unity which kept them upright; they were in solidarity not so much by close proximity but a shared experience of dignified, silent despair within their coal tarnished walls.

It was on my history course that I met my next narcissistic boyfriend, like a fool who never learns. Dai (an ex-businessman) was a lot older than me, but partying with his younger mates like a teenager, which should have been a warning sign because he was around the same age as my mother's boyfriend, who was equally immature. At the time, I reasoned that even though he was divorced like Brian, unlike Brian, he kept in touch with his kids, which at least made him more responsible. I was attracted to this sense of duty after years with Brian whose only sense of duty was making, plying us with food, which didn't compensate for behaviour which was abnormal even by my introverted standards. Neither was Dai a pathological liar like Carl, but I was about to find out that deception can take many forms such as the manipulative behaviour Dai was about to display. "I love you," ventured Dai in the student union bar, one evening.

Of course, it was a trick, but I went along with it because I wanted a relationship with someone intelligent, tough and outgoing; he was someone I thought I could learn from. I had thought the same thing about Carl, too, but I had nothing to lose since I was incapable of loving him back. Yes, I did learn much from Dai, I learnt never to trust a narcissist because for all Dai's straight talk, he had still tried to trick me in the hope I would fall in requited love just to stroke his selfish ego.

Suffice to say a relationship with an overgrown teenager living in a sixties time warp didn't work out because my heart was safely stored away in my fortress. The roman fortresses in south Wales had always fascinated me since they were built with protection in mind. Yes, they were as physically and mentally restrictive as four encroaching mountains—like being placed in a stony box—but they guaranteed safety. They made you feel formidable, resolute and as stubborn as the unmoving, unmoveable walls, built to endure all enemies. Even Dai dumping me by payphone (mobiles were for yuppies or the affluent) left me unperturbed. In fact, it was a relief after his egotistic mind games. However, it opened my eyes to what was becoming more apparent in my adulthood; I was attracting the same type of bloke, which was the type my mother attracted. I must have had gullible stamped on my forehead, and I decided then that if I was ever to get involved with any more males, it would be nothing more serious than a fling. I didn't want a family anyway because it was obvious I was never going to be normal.

I had resumed my drinking in college, only this time, I was doing so in the privacy of my bedroom. I had turned from a binge drinker to a regular, secret drinker. The alcohol helped with my lifelong insomnia problem. I was well on the road to alcoholism and didn't even try to deny it myself. I was self-abusing and didn't care. There was no way I could see any doctor because I was done with being treated as some working-class idiot by men who couldn't even work out what was wrong with me. Their pomposity was even to make me scream.

After the course and a 2.2 degree, I didn't even bother looking for work because my daily drinking was causing me a slow slide into self-induced oblivion. Luckily, I had managed to move out of Brian's lair when Beth came to my rescue after buying Mum's house for £30.000 in the late nineties (a two-bedroom council property now would cost triple that amount) and recommended me as a tenant to her old landlord, who was also a family friend. My new landlord rented out the one-bedroom cottage for £40.00 a week, which was a rate he never increased as he knew Beth well. Yes, who says nepotism is a bad thing?

Gran was also benefitting from nepotism as she moved into a bungalow after jumping the waiting list because a council worker had been her neighbour and put in a recommendation for her. By complete chance, I ended up living a mile from Mum and Gran a mile from her daughter at the other end of town. The only losers were Gran's kept sheep, who would wait for her at feeding time every day for weeks after her move.

Thus three generations kept up the extended family tradition, which since the closure of the mining industry was slowly dying out. The relocation of nearly all the factories also meant that social immobility was soon to be thing of the past. The nuclear family and job migration were arriving fast to an area once slow in making social progress. Even conservative clubs were forced to allow the genders to mix in the same room. Ex-miners could no longer justify club policy's based on machismo and sexism when many of the male folk were either unemployed or working in the same offices as women.

I had ended up living next to an ex-miner, who had worked in a mine owned by his dad. The man's father had exploited his son so badly that his son still longed to kill him. Despite my neighbour's financial turmoil, he had managed to get away from his dad and start afresh. In spite of being an ex-boxer, he was a dignified guy, who avoided conflict and solved disputes with reason and humour, which all miners armed themselves with in order to survive the daily ordeal of avoiding eye contact with one's fellow workmates. Then there were the potential hazards of being trapped down a mine overnight, which had driven one miner insane. I learned a lot from my humble neighbour about surviving against the odds, which was a lesson I was about to need.

My neighbour, on the other side of my home, had been a member of the political group, Owain Glyndwr, back in the eighties, which had been responsible for arsons on holiday cottages throughout Wales. These second homes bought by outsiders pushed up property prices to a level, locals—in deprived regions—couldn't afford. Even though their actions were extreme there were economic reasons behind the militancy. Whatever one thinks of my colourful neighbours, they were friendly and helpful. I soon settled into my terraced, slate coated cottage, in which I watched the world change as student loans replaced grants; the age of the web or goggle was fully established (Facebook was yet to make its mark) and mobiles (not smartphones) were starting to get popular. Trouble was, I was getting rigidly stuck in a beer-drenched rut, which was causing me to isolate myself more and more from the world outside my concrete shell.

My sole visitor to my cottage was Gran (apart from one

visit by my mother) and it was while we were watching a film, one evening, which was curtly titled, Beloved—the biopic of Beethoven's life—that I developed a love for opera music. My taste in music had progressed from disco as a kid; rock as a teenager and in my twenties, opera. Beethoven more than any other composer gave me solace from his own struggles with deafness, which had destroyed all his relationships as he was forced to exist in a world which did not understand him. I was touched by the trials of a man who was able to transform the pain of an invisible disability into stunning works of art. Bizarre as it sounds, I could relate to the frustration of living in a maze of confusion with all its terrifying twists and turns, which more adventurous folk would find thrilling. Of course, I don't know what it feels like to be deaf, but I knew what it felt like to be shunned, mocked and loathed even if I didn't know why. However, it had all taught me to be sympathetic to the plight of outsiders, who lived on the cusp of society like spiders taking shelter from the fearful.

I was soon to experience my own dose of unreasonable panic when I was in bed one night. I heard someone furiously pulling on the front door handle from the outside for a few minutes. I couldn't even dash to the window or move from the bed, and making the short trip to the bathroom, which was the only room in the open-plan house with a door, was impossible with clay feet lodged stubbornly on the mattress. Abject terror had taken over my whole body, making it heavy as it refused to listen to the mind telling it to react. Instead, it remained so still that only my ears still functioned. Thankfully, the possible intruder gave up, leaving me to imagine the worst-case scenario. Why would anyone try to break in a tiny cottage? My TV was the old box-shaped TV before flatscreens or digital boxes, and that was about the only electronic device in a building where a shower had never been installed. There wasn't even a microwave, cooker or washing machine in sight. The conclusion I inevitably came to was that it was me the trespasser was after. Of course, this dramatic assumption may have been an over-reaction on my part, but that's what fear does to you.

The horror of the night before hit me full on one morning as I struggled to get out of bed; I just didn't want to face the day. Unable to even motivate myself to even reach the kettle, I sat frozen solid on my sofa being assaulted by the most negative images, which mentally paralysed me. Bizarre images flew like circling vultures into my fevered brain of strange, hooded, faceless men racing up my stairs towards my bedroom as I lay crouched under my duvet. They surrounded me, prodding and poking my trembling figure as even my dried up mouth clammed shut in fright. The image was repeated over and over in my head without any resolution because my imagination refused to confront them. They were too monstrous to confront, and worse of all, they were rooted in my fantasy as firmly as weeds dig in when a gardener makes a feeble attempt to remove them. The illusionary rapists were not going to be ejected from my mind without a fight. I knew if I didn't do something drastic, they were going to take over my every waking hour, becoming more and more real until I suffered a psychotic breakdown.

Breakdowns were common in the area because of the deprivation, also—I believe—because that whilst the mountains gave the valley a well-defined structure, it did not structure our lives. In actual fact, folks' lives often fell apart within our geographical confines, which seemed to make the behaviour of neighbours intrusive and privacy difficult. I often wished that our heroic dragon would rush down from his hidden lair and breathe some fiery life into the apathetic, the despairing and the agonised. Alas, our heroine had abandoned us to our wretched drugs and alcohol; she stayed as a god on the summit of some mount looking down on us and laughing at lives infused with wanton self-destruction.

I was determined not to succumb to my invisible, soul-destroying anguish. It took me all day to extract the molesters just by focusing all my thoughts on my ex-miner neighbour. I told myself over and over why are letting a minor incident plague your every moment when your mate next door was brutalised by his mentally ill mother; he was conned by his father and friend; he was robbed by a sister and ended up married to a woman as violent as his mother? He even spent a short while on the streets and nearly froze to death until he got his life back on the proverbial track. If he could come through all that then you can brush off something lesser, which may have another explanation such as a drunk going to the wrong door.

My neighbour saved me from a steady mental decline without ever knowing it. All his tribulations became my shield from images, which I had allowed to mushroom in the darkest spots of my imagination like uncontained fungi. I was annoyed with myself for leaving the images gleefully run riot. I had started to be afraid of the real world and this had to stop.

I made sure I saw my mother each day, who was having troubles of her own with the now-retired Brian. Retirement was giving Brian the opportunity to control every aspect of Mum's life, which he was unable to do while in full-time employment with the council and doing hobbling work in his spare time. His control was causing her constant stress. Brian had never been a domestic abuser in the strictest sense of the definition back then, which was a spouse beater. You have got to take into account that marital rape wasn't even criminalised until 1991, and as for terms such as 'cohesive control', well, that were non-existent. A controlling guy might be a bully, but legally he was doing nothing wrong, which meant that Mum's mates didn't get involved, and she didn't dare tell Gran, who was already fretting over my suicidal grandfather. Before she could have kicked him out of her first home, but since they had bought another home together with joint ownership, it would be difficult to get rid. There was no way she would persuade him to sell his share of the property, especially when he had Mum to do everything, even put out the trash. His sole household chore was making mash molehills smothered in a drippy gravy unrestrained by the plates' soggy rim. I half expected a mole to escape from the mash pile.

By this time, they had married solely for tax reasons in a register office without any hint of romance as there was no point pretending it was anything other than a marriage of convenience. As for me, it was an excuse to get drunk in public under the respectable cover that the event provided. The only other time I did so in public was on Christmas day at a nearby club, open just for a couple of hours. I could enjoy drinking with all the neighbours once a year without looking like the pathetic lush I had turned into.

I was my mother's sole confidant, which sounds strange in a close-knit community, but one which has at its centre a non-stop, well-oiled gossip machine. The gossip machine is attached to an equally well-fed flimflam machine, both of which had a mutual dependency on each other. If either one ground to a sudden halt then an unprecedented muteness would descend on the town, which would quickly be followed by alarming hysteria. Besides her terror of fuelling the gossip beast, Mum's mates were also his mates at the clubs they frequented together. In short, there was no one you could really trust. Everybody had turned a blind eye to his eyeballing all the single women, his swearing and lurid remarks. If they were talking about his seedy exploits, they were doing so behind her back. However, if Mum thought he had been a social menace before his retirement, then she was in for a shock as his tyranny took hold with a vengeance.

The nineties were meandering slowly into the millennium era with the dawn of social media and all its implications for the town's maligned gossips, troublemakers and poison pen letter writers. A gossip had once said to Mum, "Don't worry, your secret won't leave the valley!"

Well, that truthful jest was about to be challenged by Facebook. There would be even more trying times ahead as folk realised that the towering slopes could no longer protect their secrets.

Questions Answered

After the excitement of the new millennium, war raged across the former Yugoslavia, but one joke came out of the tragedy at the expense of Brian, who was watching a programme on Serbia with his friend and Mum.

Brian asked his friend, "Where do the Serbs live? Suburbia?"

His enquiry provoked laughter from his mate, whereas Mum cringed inwardly. Poor Mum had cringed in silence for decades, and I couldn't fathom out how she had ended up with a controlling moron, who wouldn't leave her go anywhere alone. It was not as if it was karmic retribution for any crimes since she was the opposite of him in every way.

My mum was as friendly, generous, thoughtful, empathetic and compassionate as he was aloof, mean, selfish, un-empathetic and uncompassionate. To sum up Brian, just think of any good word and then place an 'un' in front of it, which made me wonder why he cooked us including Gran food. Then someone on the TV mentioned the term 'grooming', which I did research into and found out about 'wilful compliance', which is similar; it was the first stage of his control technique. Brian had offered Mum affection initially (I won't use the word love) and me objects or a surplus of food. We had complied wilfully in our vulnerable situation, then, later on, paid the price for it in his irrational jealousy, his drunken rages, his relentless criticism (when we weren't getting the silent treatment) and his attempts to isolate her from me. I ignored his unwelcoming attitude and visited her regularly.

Brian was never physically, though his verbal onslaughts were more insidious somehow because gradually they wore my mother down; she was being bombarded with ceaseless negative energy, which permeated every room as the angry vibes bounced off him and charged towards her. I could feel the festering animosity waiting to pounce like some movie monster lurking about unseen until it's too late.

What I am saying is probably not news to most folk, but what I will add to all the above is that living constantly with a person who is unsupportive and unsympathetic is also emotionally draining. Brian never discussed his feelings and didn't care about anyone else's. If he upset us, it was always our fault, and to my knowledge, he has never apologised for any offence in his life; I don't believe he is capable of any remorse. Living with someone so inhuman is unbelievably trying for the simple reason that you are on your own since your so-called partner is little more than a psychic vampire feeding off your (stressed) energy until one is mentally burnt out and physically sick. The malevolence has penetrated the stomach. This sounds somewhat melodramatic until I point out that Mum started to suffer from upset stomachs after every tantrum. The reader will remember me stating in a previous chapter that school bullying caused me frequent stomach aches as though all the day's tension was being stored in my digestive system until it was disrupted by an overload of stress. If a few years could do that to me just imagine decades of it knowing there will be no intervention until one dies.

We were mere energy batteries to his psychic leech, and what made it all the worse was the injustice of it. My mother had been lumbered with two self-involved men, whereas I had been, firstly, deprived of a biological father, before being stuck with a stepdad, whose only attention towards me had been lecherous as a teenager and hateful in later years. I didn't care less about his baleful glares from his armchair because I was more resentful of being robbed of a protective dad. My mother had tried to protect me in school, though she was up against the misogyny of our Head which a male figure wouldn't have encountered. A male would have been the Head's equal and as such wouldn't have run into the dead ends which surrounded all women in the area back then. I was filled with a sense of despair knowing that a masculine vacuum in our lives had created a damaging imbalance just as any imbalance leaves any person feeling incomplete, a person not whole and missing certain traits whilst growing up such as aggression. I was a yin without the complimentary force of yang. I was darkness without light to pierce the stagnation. Put simply, I had not fulfilled my full potential, which is my biggest regret in life. The fact that I had never properly rebelled because there was no role model to rebel against, said it all.

There is now the concept of and legal definition of 'cohesive control', which came too late for us. The term 'domestic abuse', back then, was way too limited and as such limiting to the likes of Mum, who couldn't even mentally conceive of her predicament in such a way. We knew he was a bully, although we wouldn't have gone as far as to call it spousal abuse. Even if we had, the rest of society wouldn't have agreed with us, thus we were to remain unprotected legally. My sole protection was my wasted education which had imbued me with the confidence to critique others, instead of myself. As I picked apart Brian, I came to the conclusion that Brian was the living embodiment of the Narcissus character I had read about as a child. Unfortunately, Narcissus had starved himself to death, which was a fate unlikely to befall orally fixated Brian, who was either chewing, smoking or drinking. It came as no surprise to learn from someone who knew his deceased mother that Brian had been spoilt. What attracted him to my mother was her single status, her lack of self-esteem, her inability to read others, we will never know.

The only certain thing was that her lack of self-belief had stopped her from leaving him. My mother's selflessness was at odds with Brian's self-righteousness which was only matched by his belligerence. You would think the two contrasting traits could not sit together in harmony, but anything is possible when the hypocrite projects his cruelty on those around him. Thus we became the problem for a self-deluded cretin, who honestly believed that we were ruining his life with our complaints. I tried not to complain too much knowing my mum would bear the brunt of his wrath. Brian had learned to use her as a weapon against me in his arsenal of brutal manipulation, which is more complex than a battery and just as devastating in its long term effect.

When I found her secret voodoo doll, one day, I had to cackle at the crude, tick-tack representation of Brian with its spindly legs beneath a protruding beer belly. The only clue that it was Brian was the photo superimposed onto the flat face. In spite of multiple pins in the chest, Brian stayed healthy, probably because the pins were impaling his heartless chest. I didn't know whether to laugh or cry: laugh that Brian with his phobia of witches had driven Mum to witchcraft or cry that he thrived through all the malice directed at him. I even believed that he would outlive both of us after being the cause of our untimely demise.

My sweet revenge was totally unintentional while they were away in Italy. I was house sitting in the evening and needed to defecate. The council had switched off the water supply for the day due to maintenance work on the water pipes. Then I remembered that there was a bottle of spring water kept in a cupboard, which I used to flush the faeces away. I thought no more of it until a furious Brian demanded to know what I had done with his vodka on his return from Italy. As it turns out, he had placed the vodka in a spring water bottle on a previous trip to the Costa Del Sol. Brian always brought back vodka from Spain, but that time he bought too much and was trying to fool customs by slipping through an extra bottle, which he would sell to mates.

So, I had accidentally poured a bottle of vodka down the toilet. I was called everything, I didn't care. What made his comeuppance so joyous was that I had enraged him whilst trying to do a good deed. It didn't occur to him that really it was his fault for devising such a silly scam on customs out of greed.

If I am being unchristian in my harsh depiction of a character beyond redemption, it's because I do believe some folk cannot be redeemed if they are lacking basic virtues such as guilt. The truth was we should not even have given him the first chance, never mind the umpteen chances over the decades which only served to entrench us even further in the victimhood of our own making. Gran's philosophy of ignoring faults in others had rubbed off onto Mum; it had turned into a family curse, which I felt was up to me to break. My mission in life was to stay single, undefeated and unbroken.

I developed strategies to deal with a situation in which I felt trapped, sort of defence mechanisms, which to others may sound bizarre. I got into birth date astrology after reading a Hindu book about the link between karma and astrology, which didn't provide me with any answers. Yes, it accurately described my personality as an uncommunicative type with unexpressed rage, but all the misfortune it couldn't explain away.

The astrological chart was like reading some script of my life, which was not a script I had given permission to. It could have been written by some vicious scriptwriter without my best interests in mind. I noted with grim satisfaction that I had managed to overcome my inability to express emotion by writing down my angst, yet I was still what some had called a reserved person (if they were being kind). However, at that moment, I was far from emotionally controlled. On the contrary, I wanted to tear it up in a fit of petulance. I desperately wanted to rewrite it something which I had not agreed to, but like everything else, in my life, I was lumbered with it. I had to convince myself that all the crap around me was karmic in nature because I wanted to be doing a lifetime of penance for a reason like some past life misdeed. I could accept a punishment which had been deemed fitting by a higher power. I still believe in divinity, and that all our lives are in the hands of a supreme power, but in a sacred text either Hindu or Buddhist could I find answers. I felt like I had been sent to prison without committing the crime, and there was no justice coming to me. In fact, my life felt like a cosmic joke without reason or rhyme. I couldn't just accept things for what they were and continued looking for answers before bitterness overcame me.

I went into past like recall hypnosis, which brought up a past life in Victorian Wales. I even managed to trace the person I may have been online, although finding out details of a previous life, which was pure to the point of being humdrum, bore no connection to my contemporary life woes. Once again, I was coming up against a blank wall with all the frustrations which it brought up. I was going to have to wait for an answer to pop up in an unexpected place year down the line. Meanwhile, I had to keep all tribulations to myself as I became intensely private for my mum's sake as well as my own, as Facebook increased in popularity in a place where rumours had always spread with a speed that a boy racer would envy.

Outside our family dramas, Facebook was becoming established slowly in an area which had once valued privacy. I had no intention of trashing my private life, nor inventing some glorious online persona. If Gran had instilled one piece of wisdom in me, it was being mysterious with an almost Greta Garbo-like zeal. The younger reader wouldn't be fans or the film star, who shrouded her life in a type of seclusion which today would be regarded with pity, even disdain. But there is something to say for the life of a hermit, who may have gained insights away from the scrutiny of the envious. I bring up Garbo because it occurs to me how much society has changed that the mystique of a recluse has been replaced by suspicion towards a loner. I knew folk perceived me as odd, but I didn't care, and I wouldn't be pressurised into making myself available to the gossips. Being elusive and mysterious had protected me over the years, and when a mate had once called me enigmatic I was not insulted for the simple reason that the perception of me as haughty had concealed all my anxieties even if it was somewhat unfair.

Not only was I and others of the older generation in danger of losing our carefully constructed facades, but thanks to Facebook, the savagery of hate mail writers, braggarts and liars had been taken to a new level. I was not going to make myself an easy target for their unworthy inspection just to be popular; I was used to being disliked all my life. The scorn of others deemed normal had done me a favour; it had set me free from the need to conform. My nonconformity was no choice since it had been pushed onto me by a society demanding I be extroverted, friendly, glamorous, married and maternal. I was never going to fulfil the above criteria, in which case, Facebook was not for me; it would have highlighted my social inadequacy.

Besides, there was no face from the past I wanted to reengage with, also I didn't really need to look up school colleagues where I lived as I often bumped into old friends/fiends in the street. Most of whom acted chummily, but I would pretend not to remember them since it didn't seem appropriate to bring up past injuries decades later. I had never been confrontational anyway, preferring the dismissive approach towards enemies. Time had not mellowed my bitterness, but I was damned if I was going to show it. Even when one moved into the same street as me, I carefully avoided her. I was still a misfit in their eyes, but it had taught me to sympathise with others in my predicament.

My single, childless, maladjusted status had taught me to make some interesting friends on my drinking jaunts. One of whom was a Romany lady called Jodie, who was single like me. Jodie had grown up on a Romany camp in a family speaking Romany, and where all kinds of spells went on. I had toyed with the idea of her putting a jink on Brian until I realised that any loss in his finances would impact on my mother since her savings were joined with his. To be fair, to the Romany folk, their spells are mostly love, money and health spells. Besides, my mother had dabbled unsuccessfully with the occult in spite of her chapel background. The truth is that most people will try anything when feeling nearly isolated, especially when the entrapment takes place in the midst of happy couples. Jodie's unique background fascinated me; she was different, like me. I was attracted to those living in society, yet never quite became part of it. I had always sympathised with certain villains because if I had been the rebellious type, I would have gone down a dark route without any support network to curtail me. History has shown that different types such as gays have been criminalised just for being deviant by nature or rather deviating from the norm. Well, I was deviant for as long as I could remember. Looking back at the unsympathetic attitude of the school bullies even my family, it was only my passivity which stopped me from getting into trouble.

Jodie, like me, had suffered so much bullying that she had left school at sixteen to marry and never worked. Jodie had left her Romany community to marry an outsider, and never returned to the Romany life, not even tempted. Jodie had been brave enough to divorce her abusive husband, whose abuse had caused her to be briefly institutionalised. I admired the way she had made a fresh start far away from all the trauma, whereas I stayed ensnared in my own snake pit. I liked a friend who brought some diversity into a community whose approach to the perverse nail, which dared to jut out rudely, was to hammer it into place.

Jodie took my mind off my own problems, which I was about to be reminded of. My self-ruin was brought home to me when Aunt Lyn died in her sleep in her own room; it was Gran and Mum who discovered her corpse, while Rhys was out, and it was them who arranged her funeral. Aunt Lyn wanted the service held in her local chapel in Welsh; she was to be buried next to her parents' double grave in a spare plot intended to create a family resting place. Aunt Lyn had died after a lifetime of doing what she wanted and travelling extensively upon her retirement; she had been a feminist before the concept existed due to a combination of intellect and determination. Yet she ended up a family woman living with her brother after her career, whose bond with her sister remained undiminished by separation. In many ways, she was a living paradox: diminutive but imposing; self-possessed but unselfish; career orientated but family-minded. In short, she was everything I was not. My aunt had infallibility about her, which I couldn't hope to emulate.

Her funeral threw up a surprise in the hulking form of my now-retired Head, who apparently attended the same chapel. Neither Mum nor I spoke to him, and his presence there made me glad that I had never been a chapel goer. Even god-fearing Gran hadn't attended chapel since a child after she had caught the preacher out in a lie. Gran loathed the chapel attendees also after hearing them disparage their neighbours outside the chapel. In spite of their hypocrisy, Gran still didn't want to see the bad in folk, whereas the day of Lyn's funeral I felt overwhelmed by its stench, and was glad when the service finished. I was even more pleased when Lyn's friend informed us that without funding from the deceased Lyn, the chapel would soon be shut. On the one hand, the chapel had kept alive the faltering Welsh language, on the other, the nature of the vale dwellers had turned it from a spiritual sanctuary to a den of gossip under the guise of false piety.

Uncle Rhys was the most distraught since he had lost a companion, cleaner and cook. It would now be up to Gran to see to his needs, and if Gran fell sick, the family duty would fall on my mother. Rhys was the spoilt baby of the family, who had always been surrounded by his family; he even spent Saturday evenings in the local with his brother-in-law. Rhys had always been fortunate that to have been brought up in a time when the community was still close-knit, and most folks were surrounded by their extended family. Even though Gran had moved, she was still only a fifteen-minute drive from his home, whose only modern installations were a washing machine, shower and gas fire. His village was still uniformly white, but with a few English and European dwellers. The homogenous tribal culture of the past was long gone, however, it had benefitted my uncle, who had been accepted as one of the miners.

When my grandfather died a couple of years after Lyn, I felt no great loss or indeed any emotional loss for a man I barely knew. I never enjoyed a proper conversation with a person who remained an enigma until the end. I don't think Mum did either, or even Gran. Granddad had kept up the miner's reserve even when ailing with coal dust induced lung disease. I felt no sadness on his passing, and attending his funeral was like watching service for a stranger. I didn't even care that he had spent his last years so suicidal that he attempted to throw himself off a bridge known locally as a suicide hotspot. I never understood why suicides were drawn to the local bridges until I read Welsh mythology regarding the devil's bridge in mid and south Wales.

Legend has it that the devil would be waiting for the unwary on the other side of the bridge, waiting to claim their souls. The devil also had an annoying habit of turning up on mountains at night time to steal souls of those foolish enough to climb mountains at night. Why pristine peaks and harmless bridges became the devil's stomping ground is an unsolved mystery, which only distant ancestors could explain. The bridges may belong to the devil, whereas many rivers in Wales are named after the pagan goddesses, which makes the Welsh landscape a balanced polarity where masculine and feminine, evil and good meet and sometimes merge. If you think about it too deeply, the (mainly male) suiciders throw themselves from a masculinised domain in order to be reclaimed by the feminised river. If they saw the river in its true light, they might think twice before jumping into their watery grave. They would probably prefer to die on the windy common of an inhospitable mount, which would be a macho ending. Anyway, Gran departed from Earth a few years after Granddad in unacceptable circumstances. The hospital had sent her back to her nursing home before her full recovery from pneumonia, which had caused her to die in her room a day later. My mother had pressed for compensation only for Gran's medical records to vanish forever, which made any lawsuit against them impossible. In a rotten nutshell, they had killed Gran and got away with it. My mum's helplessness compounded her grief on losing not just a parent, but also a friend who she had seen every day for nearly forty years.

I was less grief-stricken for a woman who had always regarded me as a social embarrassment, which I can't deny since I had not inherited her charm. Although had been contrasting characters, I can at least claim that she had more influence on me than aloof Granddad. I had inherited my love of gardens and wildlife from her. Even though I wouldn't feed a hedgehog with chicken, I would get them off the road along with frogs. I even loved seeing the occasional lizard in my garden. I had a respect for all of nature even mice and bats. I preferred listening to the squeak of a bat to any music; I will even state that living near a woods had kept my sanity intact in times when I questioned my miserable existence.

The only thing that Gran had tried and failed to instil into me was the need to be popular. Gran had treated life like it was a popularity contest with an obsessive desire to be liked by everyone, which may have been necessary when life in her village was once tribal. I knew from an early age that I was never going to be popular even with my own kind. I had never tried because it was obvious that I was meant to be different because of some cruel trick of nature, and I was about to find out the name of the trick.

My discovery came just by chance after years of visiting a hairdresser, who had a daughter in a special needs school. Her daughter had been placed there after severe bullying in a mainstream school, which she found impossible to confront. The poor girl wouldn't even defend herself when beaten savagely without provocation on her part.

On hearing that the girl had never dealt with the bullying my suspicion was raised. I had met the girl once and she seemed docile. I couldn't imagine that she would do anything to provoke anyone. The girl was slow in speech but polite and well mannered. Apart from her over-eating, she was a model child, yet a target for any bully she came into contact with. My hairdresser mentioned the words 'Asperger's Syndrome' which was a medical term I was aware of from various newspaper articles. One article had been about a girl with an IQ of 120, who would throw tantrums if classroom furniture was moved around. Even though I liked everything in its rightful place, I had never thrown a tantrum. The articles vaguely resembled my childhood concerns such as needing order and familiar patterns in life i.e. a dislike of change. However, the kids differed from me in other respects, therefore I had dismissed what I was reading as unrelated to my own eccentric behaviour, eccentric being a word my mum once called me. I didn't mind being referred to as odd, after all, I had been called weird by a junkie living on my street. I was used to being reviled; it had made me develop a tougher skin.

However, beneath my emotional composure, there was always the feeling that some unnamed condition was stopping me from reaching my full potential in life by imposing invisible constraints on a personality which had never fully developed. It had caused me to self-medicate by drinking every night in order to deal with the everyday stress of interacting with a brash world; it had sort of ruined my life. At approaching the milestone birthday of forty with the bleak but undeniable realisation that I had squandered half of my life it was finally time to find out where I had gone wrong. A medical revelation was not going to solve anything anymore, though it would at least stop me from reproaching myself for being a hopeless, reclusive drunk who couldn't keep a job or make friends. Any friends I had managed to make were social rejects like myself. I had learned about the dark of society in their treatment of misfits, but I wanted to sit down with someone who would tell me that all the rejection was not my fault. I had done nothing to warrant being treated as some snob, oddity or even vile person. I had allowed others to define me as pretentious since it was a cover for my shyness, even if it meant that I had struggled to find my own identity. Finally, it was time I started to self-define if I was ever to gain any self-worth.

Suffice to say, I went for an Asperger's Syndrome test with my mum, who had always been aware of my problems, before I was. My mum being blamed for my social retardation at my school had been burdened with guilt, which she needed relief from. I had never blamed her, but I knew that back then there were plenty of bigots in the region who had seen a single-parent mother as unfit for motherhood and saw evidence for this belief in my lack of social airs. I knew that Mum had often been reprimanded for my unfriendliness by neighbours. I didn't care, yet I knew that my supposed ignorance was reflecting badly on her mothering skills. Bearing this in mind, she deserved a diagnosis, too, since she had suffered with me.

At the age of forty, I was diagnosed with Asperger's by a psychiatrist, who offered me no support for my condition. There was a leaflet in his waiting room, which unhelpfully stated that the cause of the condition is unknown, with theories ranging from nature (genetics) to nurture i.e. a cold parent who has failed to properly bond with their child. This is a myth since I always knew my mum cared for me behind all her frustrations of rearing an abnormal child alone.

The truth was, I was still being let down by the clueless medical establishment, but at last, I had been given something I could ponder on as I came to terms with my self-discovery. My thoughts quickly turned to my Uncle Rhys, who had become more reclusive upon the deaths of Aunt Lyn and Gran. Apart from Mum and one life-long friend, he had no one, which didn't seem to bother him. Uncle Rhys had never complained of loneliness and even seemed contented living a secluded existence, which would have driven others insane. I could see myself ending up like him, and if my drinking wasn't forcing me to go out, I too would have been sinking into a corner of my living room with the TV as my only companion. Of course, my uncle had benefitted from the protection of a respectable family in a village where a few males lived with their parents until their parents died. This idiosyncratic behaviour was acceptable when miners were being spoiled by their doting mums. My uncle had been fortunate enough to be in the right place at the right time.

My uncle was also fortunate that he had been reared by such a loving family, who had no trace of malice, sadness, resentment nor a personality disorder. It made no difference to his disability of course, but his happier start in life meant that he was less likely to develop a mental illness or turn to drink, which led me to the conclusion that the connection between Asperger's and depression is too simplistic. I was not prone to mental health issues simply because of Asperger's, but because I had never had the support of a functional family. There had never been a proper friend who I could confide in. There wasn't even anyone around me who I could trust. There will be those critics reading this who will argue that Uncle

Rhys still failed in life with the support of family and a close-knit tribe, although I will beg to differ. Yes, he had led a humdrum life, which could best be called dull, though the truth was this: he was happiest in his garden, and he was made to enjoy simple pleasures. He had never longed for the glamourous; he had never broken a law in his life and his only social transgressions were to remain a childless bachelor. Like me, he was built for life in the slow lane; unlike me, he had not self-destructed. Rhys's life had been as blameless as that of a monk. How many folks can say that today?

Of course, it might not have been just genetic, as Rhys was more logical than me. I also searched for clues of brain damage in my difficult birth which had involved a C-section with the use of forceps, and then water on the brain. All the above factors played their part. Even being brought up without siblings may have contributed to my love of solitude. Everything relating to my early years went against my social development. It was almost as if I was meant to be socially maladjusted. As though there was every detrimental cause bringing about one adverse effect. To use a misunderstood word it seemed karmic; it was not spiritual karma, but physical karma. Where the karma felt wrong was that ever since I had suffered through the ignorance of those around me. I had also been victimised by my own mental imbalance because my right brain had dominated the left hemisphere, which had caused me to be overwhelmed by my crazy imagination at the expense of my rational left brain. This had led to unsound decision making until I learned to ignore my vibrant fantasies. Traditionally, the right/creative/intuition hemisphere is associated with—yes, you guessed it—women. So fittingly, I always ended up surrounded by women, who I understood better than men. I was slowly getting answers even if it was somewhat too late. I was never going to change what had been thrown at me by some cruel prankster in the universe, but I was going to find out why, in order to help others in my predicament.

The Gypsy's Curse

What finally removed Rhys from his hideout in his eighties was cancer on the sole of his foot. I ought to point out that my uncle had never sunbathed been abroad and only went out in the garden in wellies. His mother had nearly died from skin cancer, who was a fair-skinned woman of Irish descent. Rhys's skin cancer came after a bout of Shingles, which had left him with scars on his back resembling burns. If it hadn't been for Mum feeding him, he would have ended up in the local hospital much sooner. Not that it mattered because the hospital was a five-minute drive from Mum's home, and one of her friends worked there.

I went with Mum to his crumbling home to pick up all his nightclothes; I did so because the place was alive with childhood memories untinged by the rigours of a miserable adolescence and disappointing adulthood. My best memories were of the lawn by the side of the caterpillar infested garden where I had once spent a summer's evening searching for an elusive four-leafed clover, a mythic luck charm. I had never questioned why a four-leafed clover would bring luck just because it is so rare. As usual, I had allowed my uncontrolled imagination to gallop off into the pixie world where magical items brought you all your wishes. When I was rewarded with actually finding one, I pressed it and kept it in my room all through luckless adolescence, until—thoroughly disillusioned—I conceded magical defeat and threw it. Maybe it was a life lesson in not being so fanciful, which I should have observed, but my enchanted right brain was not going to let me go.

At least, back then, the fantasies it churned out were all optimistic; it was as I approached middle-age, they took on a more sinister face. A gloating face which would abuse and attack me in every way in improbable environments such as public transport. Since I had always previously felt safe on buses, I have no idea why images of being bullied on a bus would suddenly invade my conscious mind while I was in bed or drinking coffee in my living room. It wasn't until I did research into OCD that I found out that as well as the positive aspect of making me a neat freak, the compulsive disorder has a negative side related to unwanted imagery or thoughts suddenly popping into your mind like some demented Jack-in-the-box jumping out of your subconscious to expose long-buried phobias. My disorder did me a favour because by confronting the junk it presented me with, I was forced to perform a psychological ritual, which would symbolically cleanse me of whatever festered beyond my conscious thinking.

I had read an autobiography written by a Hindu saint in which he described burning a birth chart as a child because it predicted a rather mundane future for a boy, whose tendencies were already leaning towards the mystical. The future yogi decided to rid himself of a future of marriage and family by symbolically destroying the prediction. As a man, he went on to become a famous Western sage in the West. I was inspired to do the same. I was no mystic, and burning my birth chart was intended only as a psychological release from the subconscious elements highlighted in the chart such as the star signs and planets in house twelve, which I considered to be inauspiciously placed. Yes, it may sound crazy to the reader, but it was just a simple ritual with no harm done.

For those readers unfamiliar with the mysterious functioning of the unconscious, I will briefly explain that the subconscious mind is accessed through rituals involving symbols such as planets, which sound magical, but when you understand the workings of the hidden section of the mind it is just bypassing the chattering of the conscious mind to gain quick access to another mental layer just like hypnosis is used to break harmful habits. It is also cheaper than hypnosis and it is less time-consuming than therapy. I burnt the chart which was a symbolic representation of my darkest fears as well as my greatest gift: my imagination, which had turned against me with such ferocity that it had become a foe. What was so paradoxical about the chaos engulfing a once ordered mind was that I was still a neat freak, and my tidy home in no way reflected the emotional clutter burying my reasoning faculties, or what remained of them.

As I watched the chart disintegrate, I told myself that the karma contents of the chart were burning with it. I didn't expect results overnight knowing that my repetitive thoughts and fantasies, especially the destructive ones, would take years to break. They were just like addictions, which started out pleasurable until they got you where they wanted, in their sweaty grasp. The important thing is that I was doing something active against my compulsions, which had taken my peace and threatened my sanity. Put simply, I was in a crazed circle of self-torture. The process of how I left the land of pixies and found myself being whipped mercilessly by a sadistic tormentor in a dungeon of my own creation was a long and steady path, which had taken me passed many traumatic events. These had inevitably coloured my outlook, but worse, my prized asset was now a hideous monster mocking me from the shadows of my mind.

Anyway, enough about my self-inflicted problems, which you must find as tiresome as I do. Back to Rhys, he was liberated from his damp abode, where he would rather face mould than leave for somewhere unfamiliar; he had been comfortably wedged into a rut by design. However, it was still up to Mum to visit him daily out of duty to Gran, who had worried about Rhys after her days. There was another reason Mum wanted to visit him: it was the one place where she was allowed out on her own without being chaperoned by Brian. The twit must have figured that she was unlikely to meet another guy on the geriatric ward. This gave her thirty minutes a day of mental and physical liberty from his control and his manipulative behaviour, such as the accusations of her flirting with mutual male mates, which he thought justified his jealous tendencies. Hence it was her fault if her freedom was restricted because she was deemed untrustworthy in his baleful eyes. These eyes took in every move and were the source of his puny power. Mum's visits had nothing to do caring for Rhys because of his foolishness.

Firstly, Rhys had taken Mum aside at her wedding reception, years earlier, and asked her point-blank, 'Why are you marrying him?'

The disapproval in his question stunned Mum, she was aware of his dislike of Brian, yet still shocked that he would voice his disdain at such an inappropriate time. Rhys was normally a cautious man more reserved than me, but when he did choose to open his gob, he did so in the wrong place. Maybe the emotive event had brought out an unknown rash streak in him, but it had ruined Mum's day. Their bond was severed by several careless words.

Secondly, when Mum collected clothes from his bedroom, she could find no trace of the valuable grandfather clock—once seated downstairs—upstairs. Neither were there any signs of antique paintings, missing for years, in any room. Mum had always assumed that he had stored them either in a spare room since he couldn't reach the attic. When asked, Rhys admitted that believing them to be worthless, he had thrown them in the river. Mum inwardly seethed; he was too old to be yelled at so she had to leave the matter drop. We have no idea about the true value of all that was thrown, even if they had been worthless, Rhys had lacked the common sense to give them to charity; it was his stupidity that annoyed us the most. There was no point dwelling on spilt milk or, in his case, tossed away the cream.

Rhys's cancer had spread too far to be treated, but that didn't stop callous doctors suggesting an amputation when it had reached his groin area. The amputation would have included the whole of his right buttocks and leg. Not to rid him of the disease but as a pain relief measure. My uncle was nearly ninety-years-old and too drugged to give his consent. The risk of such a major procedure on a pensioner was such that Mum refused without entertaining the dire notion. In truth, Mum was finished with doctors anyway; she would respect them, but the time of treating them as her superiors after what they did to Gran was over. Mum had finally learned a lesson about being too trusting of authority figures, who had never treated her as an equal because she was uneducated.

If mother couldn't visit him, I would take her place because he was the last of my extended family, apart for second cousins in a nearby village, who are from the middle-class, Anglican side of our family, and never bothered much with us, but had done well in life. I didn't grudge them this, but I can't bring myself to call them proper relatives. After all, I was from the wrong class, which no amount of education can change. I was not even a working-class hero, more like a working-class drunk. I had more in common with ex-miner Rhys than boys of my own generation. Rhys passed away at ninety in his sleep just days after the doctors' amputation request, which validated Mum's decision to refuse the surgery. He had died with dignity after living a life of quiet dignity, even though it was not many folks' idea of a life. My only living relative was Mum, and she was dominated by Brian, who made my visits unpleasant.

I made the decision to find voluntary work to alleviate my boredom now that I was no longer visiting Rhys. Little did I know when I applied for work in a local charity store that I was placing myself at the mercy of another manipulative bully.

The shop in question was in the next village and was being run by a well-intentioned English lady called Maggie. Londoner Maggie reminded me of my departed Gran in her eagerness to please everyone, and her determination to see the good in everyone. I knew right away that I was going to get on well with Maggie. I had no idea then that Maggie was taking abuse from committee men because Maggie was unfailingly civil to everyone, even lazy volunteers, who took advantage of her kindness.

There was also the much tougher floor manager, Darren, who I managed to bond with because I was able to practise my bad Welsh on Darren, a fluent Welsh speaker. I had no idea at the time of how this bond was going to be crucial later on in saving my job from a notorious troublemaker. Grumpy Darren was an unlikely knight-in-shining armour, yet I was soon to need him onside as it became apparent that there was workplace politics going on behind the scenes.

There was also an all-male (chauvinist) committee filled with alpha males. I always wondered what the region's clubs and charities would do without alpha males, which had once comprised of ex-miners, or benefit cheats, one of whom had nearly bankrupted a nearby club with all his cheating. That guy had got away with it because of misplaced loyalty, which has its origins in the deep-rooted tribalism of the village. They were always the type of guys who would have been foremen or managers if they had received the right education. Some of them liked to walk up the mountains just to stare down at their neighbours below with godly supremacy. They were the types to be avoided since they were always sexist, and one racist club committee guy had gone up to a black barmaid in his club and rudely inquired, 'What's a black bastard like you doing here?'

The barmaid didn't stay long after that; she had been the only black in the entire club, although there were more black folks in the town since my upbringing, they still only made up roughly 1% of the area's population. Although there were a large population of English folk in the town most of them were white, and some had left English cities. There was a high level of migrant habitation. There were other economic reasons for them to settle in Wales i.e. free medical prescriptions, lower cost of living etc, but the fact was Wales was seen as an attractive destination for city folk because they were getting away from problems in diverse cities. Anyhow, I soon met the other volunteer, Gwen, who was given the task to train me. Gwen being older than me was also a technophobic or a techno sceptic; she was also single after a bitter divorce. Gwen seemed like a cheery, intelligent lady at first, and I grudgingly admit to being taken in by her superficial charm in spite of being a remorseless gossip. I could cope with this since not being on Facebook (she didn't even own a computer) I figured that at least any gossiping she was doing was limited to the workplace. Looking back with hindsight, I am extremely thankful for this small mercy because there is no doubt in my mind that if Gwen had been using social media it would have been a weapon with which she could have done many folk boundless damage.

My first clash with Gwen was on St David's, I had walked into the shop to find a grumpy-looking her comically dressed up in the Welsh costume, which is a costume sold usually only in Kids' sizes. I had never seen an adult dressed in the costume, and I pitied Gwen guessing that it must have been Maggie's idea as I couldn't see Gwen willingly subjecting herself to that humiliation. I wisely said nothing and stifled the urge to laugh. When it was quiet, I took a short coffee break in the corner of the store, which provoked a tantrum from Gwen, 'You do realise you could help?'

Gwen stormed off in a huff before I could answer. I was taken back by this childish scene, but I told myself, well, she is in a mood over the dress. I was trying to be sensitive to someone I saw as a friend when it would have been wiser to pull her up on her petulance. There was no way I was going to complain to Maggie, who she was always sucking up to; she was also the hardest worker there, and I was a part-time newbie. Gwen may have been sent there by the jobcentre, yes, but she had made the job her life; it had become her gossip, centre, where she could complain about her ex, other volunteers and Maggie. If Maggie had known what Gwen called her behind her back she would have been shocked.

To be fair, to Gwen, she had been sent there by the jobcentre with the stark choice of slave labour or a dole sanction, which I knew was happening to folk around me. There was no way she was going to get employment with a local business because the nepotism in the region was such that the small businesses would only employ family or friends. Yes, they had a legal obligation to advertise a job vacancy, but I knew from personal experience that they did not respond to applicants. Gwen's other disadvantage was not being able to afford a car, and buses in the rural area are not regular. Therefore Gwen was going to be stuck in unpaid work for the rest of her life, which is why I overlooked her bitterness.

Another reason I forgave her sourness was that I admired the woman at first. I had great admiration for her defiant attitude towards all the males in the charity, who she criticised as spoilt by their mothers, which I couldn't disagree with. My awe grew when she told me about the time, as a child, she had been thrown out of the chapel for asking the preacher too many questions. Gwen labelled religion as 'evil', which is too strong a word to describe institutions maybe, although I would go as far as calling Christianity un-feminist in its past treatment of women. Some might think Gwen opinionated, moralising even, which I liked at first before I realised that what I had mistaken for feminist opinions was actually old-fashioned priggishness. It was no surprise then when I caught her slagging me to a temporary worker in the storeroom. What was hurtful was that it was blatant lies, 'She doesn't do anything unless asked, and then puts everything in the wrong place!'

I should have walked straight in there to challenge such unfair comment, especially when they were being delivered, or spat out, with such unnecessary vitriol. This was more than anger it was deep-seated bitterness after I had carried all heavy items from the storeroom e.g. vases, ornaments, wooden clocks because she constantly complained of backache. I decided against making a scene, which was never my style; I was going to bid my time and have some fun with her. I was not scared of Gwen, but I was suddenly aware of all the trouble she could be causing me. I already suspected that when I put out something faulty by mistake, that Darren had noticed, that it was she who had shown it to him. Then there was the time she had accused a committeeman of stealing from other workers. Gwen had no proof of this, and the man's only error was to boss her around one day. The guy had always been cordial to me, and since she was ordering me around I wondered if he had been trying to teach her a lesson; if he was then it had been wasted on a woman unaware of how vile she was.

I got friendly with an Asperger's lad, who briefly worked there; he was immature, yet he had always been nice to me. Evan was nonaggressive, except for being passive-aggressive in the sense that he would steal small items from any folk who took advantage of his disability. Like myself, Evan bore grudges as a result of a suppressed anger which he felt unable to verbally express. Unlike me, Evan suffered from Prada-Willi, which made him a compulsive eater; he would spend much of his shift secretly scoffing food from his backpack. Poor Evan consumed food with the zeal of a rubbish lorry digesting all trash coming its way. To be fair, to the lad, I had never met an Aspie person who was not addicted to either food or drink (myself included), which I am sure resulted from the right/feminine hemisphere brain imbalance; the right-hemisphere being associated with feminine instincts and creative abilities. In my opinion, its domination over our left masculine hemisphere also attributed to our feminine greed.

The women in Welsh myth were greedy, or at least full of unbridled passions such as shrieking. They would always be seen at night haunting/terrorising the rural, lonely roads carrying jugs of milk (in Evan's case a jug of crisps, and in mine a jug of beer). So it is no coincidence that the Welsh word for the night is feminine in honour to the fierce queen of the night and all the terrors which define her wild character. Whether the fearsome hag was a Christianised/sanitised depiction of the Celtic moon goddess or owl goddess, I don't know. I got two significant points from the story: firstly, they lacked the self-control of the sun god, and secondly, the night was their domain, where all their abundance was cloaked in darkness, which was inevitably disrupted by the presence of the more restrained solar god. It is understandable then that the right-hemisphere brain has been feminised by global legends and female classical prophets.

The problem was in the case of Evan and I was that the wilful feminine was reigning supreme over the masculine hemisphere, which was causing us to inwardly implode under the strain of our over-indulgence in food or drink. Nature demands an equilibrium either in the outer world or our inner realm. Human society is another matter though because all western institutions—not to mention workplaces—require the utilisation of the left-brain to the detriment of the right-brain. In other words, the left-brain tyranny over the right is preferable to the imbalance in reverse. So much so that the likes of Evan and I were deemed disabled i.e. not fit for any purpose in a capitalist society.

I felt for Evan with his overlooked sensitivity since most folk couldn't see beyond a lad who was mentally younger than his chronological age, overweight, non-expressive and non-verbally combative. I knew some of what he had been through. Yes, my vocabulary has expanded considerably since my days as a committed mute, but that is what shrinks might call overcompensation for my unnatural reserve or introversion or lack of assertiveness, whatever you want to call it. All those playground taunts had done me a favour in that respect, as well as everyone who had just underestimated my abilities. If I hadn't been dumped in a mainstream school, I would have ended up as inarticulate as Evan.

I knew from personal experience not to dismiss Evan as human waste disposal because Evan—like me as a child before being forced to use some left brain—was in touch with his sixth sense. Evan could sense when someone was untrustworthy, for example, and he had always been wary of Gwen. Evan, unlike me, was still very much a right-brained person, who preferred to communicate from art and creativity than his undeveloped linguistic skills. His doodles were childish, yet imaginative at the same time since he drew them to tell a story or express a feeling, more than to be artistic for the sake of it. A less charitable person would describe him as a daydreamer, but there was more to Evan than that.

One day, Gwen blamed me for something I hadn't done in front of him, and Evan started to make fun of her loudly much to her irritation. I was proud of my mate that day; he had got involved in a spat that other workers stayed out of. One volunteer there always sought her out for her gossip, some of which was about me. That person must have known that she was lying about me to cause trouble, yet would listen to her anyway. I always partially blamed her friends for her pathological lying because I felt that they were fanning the sparks which flew out of her cottonmouth and giving them oxygen. In plain speech, they were feeding her lying addiction by giving her the attention she craved as well as giving her the opportunities to make mischief.

Ironically, for all her lying, snapping, shouting, condescending and backbiting she put herself out to be highly moralistic in her outlook to sexual relations and condemned a dead gran of hers for being promiscuous when alive, as well as any person she considered a thief. It occurred to me that she was accusing certain folk of stealing without proof, which made me fearful that she would accuse me of theft just to further tarnish my reputation there. It also occurred to me that if I quit she would let everyone know that I was sacked for being useless or even a thief. I was going to have to be careful about not falling out with her as some of the charity's customers were family friends. My mum would have been mortified if a respected worker accused me of stealing from a charity.

Evan would be the sole disbeliever because he had no interest in her storytelling. Evan and Darren were the only two unimpressed by the charmer in the place. Maggie and all the charity's customers she had taken in ignored contradictions in her tales. I don't blame them because I too was seduced by evil, evil is seductive no doubt. I even ignored signs that the woman was trying to turn me against Darren, whilst getting Darren to turn against me before I got into work.

Canny Evan seemed to be a bloke she could not easily manipulate, or maybe she hadn't tried since a bigot such as herself (she had once referred to Muslims as 'Pakis') wouldn't befriend a disabled person. I had never spoken to Gwen of my condition even when I trusted her. I didn't even tell Evan I was Asperger's as it was something I was still coming to terms with. I was still seeing it as an affliction, which had caused my confidence issues in turning causing social anxiety. As it turns out, I had done the right thing not confiding in her because it was obvious from her patronising tone that she had taken me for an idiot incapable of performing the simplest task.

Enough was enough, I decided to put my plan for her into action, knowing by this time that she took herself too seriously; I had learned from Brian that narcissists are full of their own self-importance. It was high time I pricked her pomposity. I started simply after finding a wooden spoon in the garage; it had been handcrafted by a neighbour with a dog carved in the spoon part. My mum had no use for it and had only bought it because she was friendly with the man, like Gran, she could never say no to a neighbour. For once, her generosity was to come in handy as it was the ideal joke gift for cat-loving Gwen. All I had to do was scribble the words, 'To Gwen, for stirring,' down the side of the long handle. Then with extra malice, I wrote her name above the image of

111

a fat dog in reference to her ugly, wrinkled face. Bitchy, yes, but well-deserved. Gwen laughed at other volunteers there, so it was time to see it; she could laugh at herself, but I wasn't going to hold my breath. I left the 'gift' on a table in her storeroom on her day off and was unsurprised to find it a day later in the trash bin.

By sheer luck, a week later, a thoughtful donor brought in an adult toy entitled, 'Backstabbers in the Office'. It was manufactured as a joke with the likes of Gwen in mind. The box contained a plastic knife, a notepad full of catty remarks and a pen. It was perfect for my plan as though someone above was involved in my unspoken war with the woman. I had been toying with the idea of leaving my book on psychopaths on her table, but the toy seemed less offensive, whilst making a similar point. I was out to offend the woman in a dismissive way if that makes sense. The psycho book was appropriate but less funny. If she had shown it to Maggie it couldn't easily be explained away as a prank.

The reaction to my 'gift' came swiftly when Maggie informed me that my five days a week were to be cut to two days, which just happened to be the two days Gwen took off. I soon found out from Evan that Maggie had tried to get me fired behind my back. I still didn't regret my actions because, by this time, she had discredited me so much that I was only staying there out of stubbornness. I also found out from my mate that it was Darren who had stopped Maggie from getting rid of me; he had saved my job for which I was grateful because I was going to stay long enough to see Gwen leave. I was determined to get the satisfaction of outstaying her there. Gwen had treated all my kindness as a weakness and taken everyone around her for mugs, not least Maggie. I was in a vengeful mood; she was not getting her way this time.

It was Josie who came to my rescue with a Gypsy spell, though Josie was wary of using curses. "You have to be so careful because it can rebound on you if it doesn't find the victim, and it will rebound on you three-fold in strength. My aunt who works as pentacles tarot card reader in a fair, travelling Britain, sells spells for the right price, which I don't agree with. I am only giving this to you because I know you are in a desperate situation, where there is no other favourable alternative. You are my friend, and I will always be loyal to you as you will always be loyal to me."

I never doubted Josie's loyalty, a level of faithfulness which I had never seen in a Welsh friend. Of course, there was Evan, but he was looking out for the Aspie girl. The particular spell was the reverse of a love spell. A love spell involves binding two candles together with the name of you and potential lover into the wax, on the day of Venus, Friday. The candles are then lit before repeating a sacred Sanskrit invocation. The two candles are then kept in a dark place away from prying eyes. In case you then tire of the magically acquired lover, there is an unbinding spell done to cause a break-up brought on by a row, which involves cutting the binding cords, whilst repeating a different invocation. The candles are, then, thrown away in separate bins, which I suppose is meant as a gesture of their permanent separation. If you are wondering what all this has to do with loveless Gwen, well I will tell you: I was going to work on the assumption that a bond-breaking ritual would work just as well on friendships as it did on affairs. I did so because Gwen's so-called friendships were all based on the dubious need for stirring more than bonding. I don't even believe that the woman was capable of true friendship in which case a powerful spell would easily work on shaky relations between her and her boss.

A week after the bond-breaking ritual, Gwen stormed out of work after a comment from Maggie and refused to go back. I felt guilty knowing that Maggie was trying to coax her star worker back to no avail, but the atmosphere immediately lightened in the absence of her tantrums and silent treatment of me. Even better, there was a god-sent week after her departure in the shape of the lovely Carys who replaced Gwen. Carys was there as a full-time paid employee after a previous store, she worked in, closed. Carys was raising two young kids, unlike Gwen who never spoke to her adult son. Crucially, Carys was always respectful towards me even when telling what to do. I was so glad that hard worker Carys proved to Maggie that Gwen was not irreplaceable.

Her graft made me feel vindicated in my removal of venous Gwen; I am not justifying my spell, which I wouldn't contemplate using again. But the truth is that a lot of good came out of a bad deed. The gossiping diminished; the negative energy was dispelled, and everyone there got on as everyone there knew their place, and never stepped out of line. Even those who had circled her for tittle-tattle did not express a desire to see her back. Nobody there, apart from Maggie, really missed Gwen. They missed her bullshit, which had nearly cost me my job. Nobody had cared that it was dangerous lies.

With Gwen gone, I was able to spend more time chatting to customers without fear of a row for shirking work, which had been a major sin in her eyes. I managed to get friendly with a Peruvian migrant called, Mary, who was married to a

Welsh man. Mary was a care worker and a staunch Catholic, who had lived in the town for decades. At the time of her arrival in town, the nationality of the immigrants was mainly European; she had been an exotic resident, though fortunately, she shared the same faith as the Irish, Spanish, Italians and Poles. Mary had managed to carve out a valuable life for herself in her adopted country because she had the ability to make friends with people from all backgrounds.

The demure, compassionate Mary would have been someone Gwen would have judged for being religious, and befriending someone Gwen would have disapproved of made me smile inwardly. For all Mary's conservatism, she possessed none of Gwen's priggery; she was humble in all ways. Meeting Mary made me realise how wrong I had been to exalt Gwen in my mind. Yes, I liked uncompromising women, but I was forced to admit that she was a self-centred individualist, not a feminist (no true feminist exploits other women, and then casually discards them). I had been unwise to see Gwen as a role model. From then, on my companions were to be modest; I have learned my lesson.

Soon there would be more foreign customers in the shop and town, even more, exotic than Mary. Wales had been declared a safe sanctuary for war refugees, which meant that Syrians were offered a safe haven in all parts of Wales including South Wales. My valley was to take about a dozen of them, and our charity was to play a part in getting the non-English speakers settled. First up, Maggie arranged a welcoming party for them in the local community centre. The party would involve locals meeting the Syrians, watching their entertainment before eating Syrian food the Syrian women had prepared. I had to admit that the food was delicious, and if a Syrian person had opened a Syrian restaurant in the town, I would have been a regular customer. The party was a great success and English language lessons were arranged for them in the community centre. There was also free children's clothes and female underwear for them in the shop. Maggie went out of her way to greet the refugees every time they visited her shop; she was an idealistic type of person, who saw the world as it should be, not as it really is. The reality close by that she didn't recognise was that there was a certain amount of outrage (as usual being stoked up by the tireless rumour machine working overtime) in town regarding the perceived special treatment they were getting such as new furniture and free taxi rides to the hospital and city's mosque.

This backlash has to be placed in the context of the town's dire deprivation worsened by the introduction of the bedroom tax in an area where all social housing is two to three bedroomed. The upheavals this created cannot be underestimated; I knew of one single woman in the village next who had to leave her two-bedroomed council flat without being able to afford a removal van. The poor woman was put through the indignity of removing all her possessions from one street to the next one using a wheelbarrow. The sight of her wheeling all her stuff down the road would have been comical if it wasn't so shocking. It was a pitiful sight even in an area where food banks are now a common vision in all chain stores and charity organisations. If the refugees were getting priority over struggling locals (such as jumping the housing waiting list), then any envy towards them could be considered justifiable by folk who already felt forgotten by a local government. The council forced them to wait at least a year for suitable accommodation.

The Syrians also had to deal with the effects of tribalism, an example being when Maggie tried to get the Syrian men voluntary work in the furniture repair department of her store. The committeemen initially agreed to this request until it was discovered that they were doing more work than the local volunteers. The committee chaps, feeling that they were showing up the locals and threatening their jobs, had Maggie to stop their charity work. Maggie did as she was told because she was no match for the bombastic males in the committee. Rightly or wrongly, they called all the shots behind the scenes. It was unfair, of course, yet the nature of tribalism dictates that one puts one's own kind before outsiders. It might seem a bit like racism, though you have to bear in mind that tribalism/nepotism thrives in the most deprived parts of Wales which historically were also the most remote. This double whammy ensured that any meagre benefits such as a cheap property were only going to be given to someone from a well-known family deemed deserving, or able to offer the benefactor something in return. Besides, going back just three generations ago, there were few incomers to the town.

I had too many worries of my own to be concerned about committee politics. Although Gwen was long gone, I still couldn't regain the trust of either Darren or Maggie. It was becoming clear that Darren had only kept me on to spite Gwen, and Maggie had let me stay because Darren persuaded her to. Gwen had already shot down my confidence with her harsh put-downs, and though I was no longer being abused it was apparent that I was not trusted to be in the storeroom alone, or even allowed to work in Carys' absence. I had to concede defeat and leave, but I did so knowing that it was not

117

a victory for Gwen; she had left under a thundery cloud, whereas I was leaving because all my considerable efforts there had been undermined by a master manipulator. Gwen had been reduced to knitting at home, which is more productive than spinning out a blanket of deception to deceive herself as much as others.

The only person who was going to miss me was the ever-faithful Evan, who had amazed me with his almost psychic ability to smell out a rat in sheep's clothing. Actually, in Gwen's case, a woman of arrested mental development in teenager's clothes. If I hadn't been so busy trying to emulate a fussy woman, then I would have seen all the warning lights blazing away every time she walked up to me with a false smile below sly, piggy eyes. I had allowed myself to be blinded by sinful pride, which had tricked me into believing that I could be friends with a perfectionist; a trickster who all the time had been looking down on me, leading me on and taking advantage of my eagerness to please her.

As I said goodbye to sweet Evan, I realised that he was a lot like me as a child before I became cynical, before I became guarded, before my view of the world became jaded. I was slightly more masculine brained than him, true. In fact, an apt way to describe it is as a glimmer of reality shining through the disturbed swirl of visions which made up the hag brain. The solar brain provided me with just enough realism to stop me from giving in to the wailing crone rattling loudly on the right side. Yes, she caused me to over-drink and dwell on imaginary fears, but she would never manage to make me completely lose my slack grip on reality.

Evan, at thirty, had somehow managed to keep intact his childlike, playful character. By doing so, he lacked male vanity, which had been kept in check by the modesty of a lad aware of his cognitive limits. Maybe because he had been more sheltered than me after receiving an early diagnosis of his condition in the nineties, which ensured a placement at a special needs school. Of course, it is always more complex than that since Evan's gender ruled out the sexist bullying that so permeates a macho culture the way rising damp creeps insidiously through a whole building. For example, if he had been born female, he would almost certainly be a target for his weight problem, possibly even more than his slow speech, which had been the case with my mate's autistic daughter.

I was just lucky that there were no junk food outlets in Wales in the decades of the seventies and early eighties, and Mum's range of cooking only extended as far as mash and fingers. Despite his constant eating, I still envied Evan for having received the support for his autism which had been unavailable to me. I wondered if I had been supported, decades earlier, would I have retained my youthful light-heartedness or mental purity. Autism, I realised in my observations of Evan, was not a static beast in the sense that it was affected by issues of age, generation, culture, gender even one's social class. There was no doubt that my communication and social skills had improved with age, and that born a generation later, I would have been leading a normal life by adulthood. There is also no doubt that being born a woman of a struggling single mother in a puritanical town had exacerbated my social anxiety. Yes, the town was proudly working-class, but my single-parent family was in the tiny minority of underclass, benefit recipients being frowned on back then. Then there is the matter of family history, which from the time of my great-gran's enslavement to her aunt, and

Gran's subsequent enslavement to her aunt (inherited slavery). The inter-generational slavery had a knock-on effect on Mum's generation, who was a people pleaser, like Gran, and as for me, well, I was a first-rate doormat. I can't blame autism for this because Evan just pleased himself. I have to admit that family trauma was playing some part in the creation of my identity. I would even go as far as to say that I identified more with abused women than autistic people. If that confuses you, then imagine how much it confuses a woman whose identity is neither fully autistic nor fully normal. Yes, I agree, I am a confirmed screw-up. Who wouldn't be? There is no point trying to make sense of such a toxic brew.

Suffice to say that all of the above factors have made their negative contribution to my life story. More importantly, they had further entrenched my deep-set self-image as an outcast. That said, if the price I had to pay for my partial involvement in the real world was a loss of my idealism, then it was a price I willingly paid. This world was not for idealists, which Gwen had proved by taking managerial power from meek Maggie. My problem, in the place, had been judgement clouded by my ego. My ego had stubbornly refused to leave somewhere knowing it wasn't wanted. My ego feared Gwen trashing its honest reputation when it wasn't around. I had to cast its insecurity aside for once because it had robbed me of my dignity as much as Gwen's abuse had.

I was forced to move on with flattened esteem, which was causing me to drink more. If I wasn't careful, I was going to be a tragic figure drinking all day and mostly in secret. I had to start getting out again, but there was no way I was doing any more charity work. I had gone into it to prove to myself (ego) that I was a valuable member of my community, and instead, it had been proven to me, that not only was I not valued, but I wasn't of use to anyone. I had learned my lesson the hardest way that life's challenges were going to remind me of my mental shortcomings. My rightful place was with other economic losers, and I soon found the most appropriate place.

A community centre's coffee morning was where I ended up meeting fellow rejects. All of the dozen, the *Dirty Dozen* members of the reject club didn't deserve their misfortune. They were all victims of the changed fortunes of valley life, which could be directly traced back to pit closures. Even the mass increase in drug-taking had come about because there were no longer any miners around to take on the dealers with their own brand of justice. The loss of the valley's miners as the menfolk sought out employment elsewhere meant a vacuum had been created, which petty criminals quickly filled. The protective males had now been replaced by predatory men.

They were folk whose despondency I just got; I got their frustrations, their sadness and their angst. I joined their group in 2018 just as Universal Credit was being rolled out from one county to another. West Glamorgan County suffered the change to the benefit's system before Powys county. I deliberately use the word suffer as not one member of my group have benefited from Universal Credit whether they were part-time workers or benefit recipients. There were tales of some of their kids being made homeless because the five-month delay in benefit payment made them unable to pay rent. They were being punished for being unemployed even though some were on the sick for a variety of genuine ailments.

I felt their disturbance acutely. After all, most of them

were patriotic Welsh folk despite the fact that Wales was being brought to its sturdy knees by public service cuts, unnecessary taxes and a change in a new 'benefit' which had been designed to admonish the undeserving poor. All in my group had a depression induced by helplessness, even worse, it was learned helplessness, which was leaping from father to son. The men had not just lost the heavy industry, they had lost their macho pride. The days of them being spoilt by mums and wives were over. As breadwinners, their pampering had been justifiable. The doting mum and wife is a relic of the industrial past, and sadly drugs are taking the place of all that the males have lost. Drugs are attracted to despair: drugs cling to despair because both leave a stain on the psyche of the traumatised. Everywhere I look, there is trauma, invisible maybe, but they're all the same. The twin poisons of trauma and depression were silent killers in the valley between, the overdoses, suicides, and every stress-related illnesses in the vale. The mental malaise could be traced back to a community which had been socially dismembered by unemployment, breakdown of the family, drugs, alcoholism, social media and every other modern plague imaginable.

As well as my morose coffee mornings, I ventured to see a craniologist, who straight away spotted that my skull was damaged, which he believed had been damaged at birth by forceps. I knew that my birth had been performed by a C-section, which would have made forceps necessary. The craniologist soon picked up on this when he noticed that the left hemisphere brain had been squished into the right-hemisphere brain. Henceforth the right-hemisphere had drained the left hemisphere of some of its blood supply as though a parasite.

The parasitical existence of the right on the left had done more than just create a mental imbalance; it had caused an over-stimulation of the right-hemisphere. In other words, the left hemisphere was simply too inadequate to halt the torrent of visual imagery bursting forth from the chaotic right-hemisphere. The left-hemisphere was occasionally able to slice through the fantastical current with an instrument of logic blunted by years of food shortage. Yes, I was brain damaged at birth by some weary midwife working the midnight shift at a cottage hospital. The woman had ruined my life with her carelessness without even knowing it.

Of course, the woman was not entirely to blame for my wrecked life since my birth situation had been brought about by my mum's self-neglect—after her marriage breakdown—during her pregnancy. This self-harm had inevitably led to the requirement of medical intervention during my birth: an intervention so forceful that its effect will stay with me forever. But an intervention made necessary by my father's callous disregard towards his pregnant wife. Really, I could argue that masculine detachment destroyed the feminine in my parents' relationship, so the feminine wreaked its revenge on my brain. Karma sure is a bitch!

Epilogue

We are all in our own private prisons where I come from whether it is the prison of autism, depression or being under the influence of a cohesive controller. Prisons, where the walls are invisible to the outer gaze, yet their effects are nonetheless felt by the prisoner, their family and their inner circle. The feeling that something isn't quite right; you are not happy with your lot in life; you are lonely even in a crowd; there is no one you can turn to who truly understands what you are going through. The relationship you are in is a trickster's illusion.

Of course, they are all different prisons with varying degrees of isolation: the autistic will be more isolated than the depressed, even the dominated wife. The abused wife does not live alone but nevertheless lives with a partner they cannot speak to on a mature level without provoking a confrontation. Therefore their frustration remains unspoken and unseen as often their abuser is unaware of the suffering they cause. If they are aware of the misery they have created, they will never acknowledge it, let alone take any responsibility.

The sad truth is that a narcissistic type is so lacking in self-awareness that it is impossible to reason with them, which means that the only solution to the spouse's situation is to leave. This may not even be possible in rural areas where there is less support for domestic abuse. Even talking to friends may not be a viable option if one has shared friends with one's partner because most older generation clubs cater to couples. Yes, it is good that the law has changed; the once strict definition of domestic abuse, yet it is too late for my mother's generation whose social life and finances are tied in with their partner. If she started alone now, she would certainly lose her friends and home; it is easier for her to stay in jail until one of them dies.

Anyone can be a target of a dominator by which I mean anyone unable to see the red flags. These flags can be flying right in one's face, and one can still be oblivious to their warning. In some cases, a woman may choose to ignore them if they have been brought up to see her future partner as a protector and provider, who will give her the fairy-tale ending that all those silly stories promise. This naivety makes a person vulnerable to predators, who hide their true intentions until the trap shuts tight.

However, it is more complex than that due to the family history of servitude running through two generations. Even low-level bondage to another robs the servant of their self-worth. If my mother had been brought up with a stronger sense of worthiness, would she have ended up with better? There is something to be said for a sense of entitlement after all, which was not just lacking in my family, but most working-class families I know. A sense of knowing one's place, which stops one from fulfilling one's true potential. More importantly, it gets lowly women/men stuck in one-way relationships.

If I can offer one piece of advice to women/men, it is this:

do not ignore the inner voice telling you that your prospective partner lives in an emotional wilderness, where no empathy, compassion and shame can flourish. If you do ignore the warnings, you are destined to not just join him/her in the wasteland, but to become a prisoner there with a con person stealing valuable energy.

On a final note: it is not just males who are guilty of control freakery since my workplace experience with a female narcissist is evidence that a fellow sister cannot just undermine, deride and abuse you but make you feel alone. The feeling of being alone in the situation is key here when a popular colleague or partner manages to isolate you; a person who seems to reserve their hatred for you and you alone. Their power comes from their ability to instil in their victim a feeling of loneliness. The legacy of a narcissist is the severing of proper relationships.

CPSIA information can be obtained
at www.ICGtesting.com
Printed in the USA
BVHW052034240821
615132BV00015BA/619

9 781398 401532